Emilie Kiser: The Untold Story
A Deep Dive into the Life, Legacy, and Impact of a Rising Star

Introduction

Emilie Kiser's name is one that has begun to resonate in various circles, and her story is one that speaks to the power of resilience, ambition, and the drive to make an impact. Born into a world where expectations often overshadow dreams, Emilie navigated the complexities of life with grace, determination, and an unyielding belief in her potential. This book is an exploration of that journey—the path she carved for herself against all odds, and the stories that shaped her into the remarkable individual she is today.

At first glance, Emilie may appear to be just another rising star—someone whose success seems to happen overnight. However, behind her rapid ascent lies a tapestry of hard work, setbacks, triumphs, and personal evolution. The narrative of her life is not defined by any one moment but rather by the culmination of decisions, relationships, and moments that forged the woman we know today.

This book, Emilie Kiser: The Untold Story, is not just a recounting of her professional accomplishments; it delves deeply into the personal side of Emilie, unearthing the events, challenges, and milestones that have shaped her character and ambitions. From her humble beginnings to becoming a force to be reckoned with in her chosen field, her journey has been one of passion, grit, and an unwavering sense of purpose. But this story is more than just a biography—it's a reflection of the universal human experience. It's about perseverance when faced with adversity, the strength to overcome self-doubt, and the courage to stand tall when the world seems to be pushing you down.

The rise of Emilie Kiser is a testament to the power of inner strength and the importance of self-belief. Her story is one of transformation—not just in terms of career achievements, but in her growth as a person. It is about how she learned to embrace vulnerability, deal with her insecurities, and use them as tools for growth rather than obstacles to her success. Through countless trials and triumphs, Emilie emerged not only as a professional success but as a symbol of resilience and hope for many who struggle to find their own paths.

As you journey through the chapters of this book, you will discover the different facets of Emilie's life that have shaped her into the person she is today. You will learn about her early influences and aspirations, the pivotal moments in her career, and the personal struggles that have molded her character. Along the way, you will gain insight into the values that drive her decisions, the relationships that have helped her grow, and the obstacles she has overcome to reach the heights she now occupies.

But this book also invites you to see Emilie Kiser from a different perspective. It offers a deeper understanding of how fame and success can impact a person's private life, how media and public perception often blur the line between the real and the imagined. By peeling back the layers of Emilie's life, we reveal not just a public figure but a person—one who experiences the same doubts, dreams, and challenges that we all face.

Ultimately, Emilie Kiser: The Untold Story is a celebration of what it means to embrace your own journey, to push forward when others may doubt you, and to discover, through perseverance and self-reflection, the power you have to shape your own destiny. This is the story of Emilie Kiser—but it's also the story of anyone who dares to dream, work tirelessly, and overcome the odds to make those dreams a reality.

Chapter 1
Early Life and Beginnings

The story of Emilie Kiser's rise to prominence begins long before the spotlight found her. Like many great figures whose impact is felt across industries, her journey to success was not marked by a singular event but rather a series of defining moments that shaped her into the person she is today. The foundations of Emilie's character, ambition, and perseverance were laid in her early life, where she navigated a world filled with challenges, dreams, and formative experiences. Her story is a reminder that every success, no matter how extraordinary, begins with humble beginnings.

Born into a family that valued hard work and resilience, Emilie was exposed to the importance of ambition from an early age. Her parents, each with their own unique backgrounds, instilled in her a strong sense of determination and the belief that anything was possible with the right mindset and work ethic. Growing up in a modest household, Emilie learned early on that success was not handed to anyone—it had to be earned. While other children may have been preoccupied with play, Emilie often found herself thinking beyond the present, envisioning a future where she could make a difference. It was within the confines of her childhood home that her desire to excel and her thirst for knowledge first began to take root.

Education became one of the cornerstones of Emilie's development. From an early age, she showed an aptitude for learning, and her curiosity about the world around her was insatiable. Whether it was diving deep into books, asking insightful questions, or participating in extracurricular activities, Emilie was constantly looking for ways to expand her horizons. Her thirst for knowledge was not limited to school subjects alone—she was equally intrigued by human nature, the complexities of relationships, and the world's intricacies, which would later serve as guiding principles in her professional and personal life.

As a young girl, Emilie was known for her persistence. While others may have been content to settle for mediocrity, Emilie always pushed herself to exceed expectations. Her teachers often noted her natural ability to grasp difficult concepts and her determination to overcome challenges. This drive was apparent not only in her academic pursuits but also in her extracurricular activities, where she dedicated herself fully to every endeavor. Whether it was sports, drama, or leadership roles in school clubs, Emilie demonstrated an unwavering commitment to excellence. However, these early successes were not without their obstacles. As an ambitious young woman, she sometimes faced resistance, both from peers and society, who doubted her abilities. But rather than allowing these doubts to hinder her, Emilie used them as fuel to push harder and prove her worth.

Her childhood was also marked by moments of self-discovery—moments when Emilie realized the importance of forging her own path, regardless of external expectations. While she faced societal pressures to follow a conventional trajectory, Emilie knew deep down that she was destined for something different, something bigger than the life others envisioned for her. This realization ignited a passion within her to pursue her dreams with a singular focus, and it set the stage for the years of hard work that would follow.

The early life of Emilie Kiser was one of challenges and triumphs, learning and unlearning, self-doubt and self-belief. It was during this formative period that she began to cultivate the values and skills that would become the foundation of her future success. The trials she faced, the lessons she learned, and the dreams she nurtured during this time were pivotal in shaping the person she would later become—a figure whose influence would extend far beyond the boundaries of her upbringing. Chapter 1 sets the stage for the remarkable journey ahead, showing how Emilie's early years provided the groundwork for the incredible story that would unfold in the chapters to come.

Family Background and Upbringing

Emilie Kiser's journey to success cannot be fully understood without delving into the roots of her family background and the values instilled in her from an early age. Like many individuals whose lives become a testament to resilience and determination, Emilie's foundation was built within the walls of her home, where the influence of her parents, siblings, and close family members shaped her character and her view of the world.

Born to a middle-class family, Emilie grew up in a household where love, respect, and hard work were emphasized above all else. Her parents were both hardworking individuals who dedicated themselves to providing for their family while nurturing an environment in which their children could thrive. Emilie's mother, a strong and independent woman, balanced her career with raising her children, teaching Emilie the importance of perseverance and the power of women in a world often slow to recognize their potential. Her father, a steady and wise figure, offered Emilie a sense of stability and strength. He was someone who valued education and believed deeply in the power of knowledge to change lives.

From the moment Emilie could walk, she was immersed in a family dynamic that emphasized the importance of education and personal growth. Her parents were committed to creating an environment that not only supported academic success but also nurtured emotional and moral development. Discussions around the dinner table were often centered on current events, philosophical questions, and ethical dilemmas, fostering an atmosphere where intellectual curiosity was encouraged. This constant engagement with thought-provoking topics helped shape Emilie into someone who would go on to question societal norms, challenge the status quo, and seek meaningful change in her own way.

While Emilie's parents instilled in her the importance of academic achievement, they also emphasized the value of kindness, empathy, and resilience. From an early age, Emilie learned that success wasn't just about earning degrees or accolades but also about developing a compassionate heart and the strength to face life's challenges head-on. Her mother, in particular, taught her to embrace her individuality and always pursue what made her happy, regardless of how unconventional it might seem to others. This allowed Emilie to explore her interests without fear of judgment, leading her to pursue passions beyond what was expected.

Siblings played a pivotal role in shaping Emilie's life as well. Growing up with her brothers and sisters, Emilie experienced the dynamics of sibling rivalry, shared successes, and the occasional challenges that come with growing up in a bustling household. Her siblings, each with their own personalities and ambitions, helped her develop important life skills such as negotiation, patience, and conflict resolution. These experiences would later help Emilie in her professional and personal relationships as she learned to navigate different perspectives and find common ground with others.

The extended family was also a significant influence in Emilie's life. Both sides of her family emphasized the importance of community, relationships, and social responsibility. Family gatherings were often filled with stories of resilience and perseverance, passed down from generations that had faced hardships but always found ways to overcome them. This sense of history and the legacy of those who came before her became a cornerstone of Emilie's outlook on life. It helped her understand that success was not solely the result of individual effort but also the product of a collective legacy—an inheritance of strength and wisdom that could be relied upon during times of difficulty.

Despite the warmth and support of her family, Emilie's upbringing was not without its struggles. Like many families, her household faced financial challenges, especially during times of economic downturns. However, these struggles only strengthened the resolve of Emilie's parents to provide the best for their children. The hardships they faced were not viewed as obstacles but as opportunities to teach resilience and resourcefulness.

Emilie's family background and upbringing were foundational in shaping her character and worldview. The love, support, and lessons from her parents, siblings, and extended family cultivated a sense of self-worth and determination that would carry her through the challenges of her life. This solid family foundation, built on values of hard work, integrity, and compassion, prepared Emilie to face the world with confidence and an unwavering belief in her ability to make a difference. The lessons she learned within the walls of her home continue to echo throughout her career and her personal journey, making her not just a success in the professional world, but a woman who embodies the very values she was raised with.

Early Influences and Aspirations

Emilie Kiser's formative years were shaped by an array of early influences that sparked her ambitions and fueled her drive to pursue something beyond the ordinary. From the stories she heard growing up to the experiences she encountered in her early education, Emilie's world was a tapestry of diverse influences that guided her toward the path of greatness. These early influences, both external and internal, planted the seeds of her future aspirations and were instrumental in shaping the person she would eventually become.

One of the most significant influences in Emilie's life was her mother. As a strong, independent woman who balanced a demanding career with raising a family, her mother became Emilie's first role model. She watched as her mother navigated the challenges of being a working professional while still maintaining a nurturing home environment. This taught Emilie the value of hard work and the importance of carving out one's own space in a world often dominated by conventional expectations of gender roles. It was through her mother's example that Emilie learned that being a woman didn't mean having to settle for less or conform to societal norms; instead, it meant finding ways to break barriers while staying true to oneself. Her mother's influence sparked a deep desire in Emilie to be more than what was expected, to pursue her passions unapologetically, and to prove that women could excel in any field they set their minds to.

In addition to her mother, Emilie was deeply influenced by her father, whose values of intellectual curiosity and a love for learning left a lasting impression. Her father's dedication to education, both formal and informal, opened Emilie's eyes to the power of knowledge and self-education. He would often take her to libraries, encouraging her to read widely and explore subjects beyond her school curriculum. This exposure to a variety of disciplines fueled Emilie's intellectual curiosity and ignited a lifelong passion for learning. She realized early on that the more she knew, the more power she had to shape her own destiny. Whether it was history, science, literature, or the arts, Emilie found herself fascinated by the world's complexity and eager to understand how she could make an impact.

In school, Emilie's natural curiosity was nurtured by teachers who saw her potential. She excelled academically, but it was not just grades that motivated her—it was the pursuit of understanding, the thrill of solving problems, and the joy of discovering new ideas. Her love for learning extended beyond the classroom, where she would often take on extracurricular activities that challenged her and allowed her to hone new skills. Whether it was joining the debate team, volunteering for community projects, or organizing school events, Emilie was constantly seeking ways to expand her horizons. These experiences helped her develop the skills of leadership, communication, and problem-solving—skills that would later become invaluable in her career.

However, Emilie's aspirations were not solely shaped by her family and academic influences; they were also fueled by a deep sense of internal motivation. As a young girl, she was drawn to the idea of making a meaningful difference in the world. She often daydreamed about creating something that would leave a lasting legacy—a company, an initiative, or a cause that would touch lives and bring about positive change. This aspiration was born from a strong sense of social responsibility that Emilie developed early on, having been raised in a family that valued compassion and service to others. She began to envision a future where she could leverage her talents and skills to help others, particularly those who were marginalized or overlooked. This internal desire to make a difference became a driving force in Emilie's life, propelling her to chase after her dreams relentlessly.

Moreover, Emilie was influenced by the growing presence of women in leadership roles during her childhood. Watching women in politics, business, and entertainment defy the odds and shatter glass ceilings inspired her to believe that she, too, could achieve greatness. These women served as living proof that ambition, hard work, and perseverance could overcome even the most deeply entrenched societal barriers. They taught Emilie that success wasn't just about what you were born into, but about the choices you made and the effort you put into shaping your future.

As Emilie matured, these early influences—family, education, and her internal drive—began to crystallize into clear aspirations. She knew that her future would not be defined by the limits others placed on her; it would be defined by the pursuit of her own passions, the knowledge she gained, and the difference she would make in the world. These aspirations set the foundation for everything that came next in her life—career choices, personal decisions, and the relentless pursuit of excellence.

Emilie's early influences and aspirations are a testament to the power of a supportive environment, intellectual curiosity, and a deeply rooted desire to leave a mark on the world. They shaped her into a person who understood the value of hard work, the importance of compassion, and the need to continually evolve and grow. These influences provided the initial spark that propelled her to dream big and strive for a future that was uniquely her own.

The First Steps in Her Journey

Every journey begins with a single step, and for Emilie Kiser, those first steps were taken at a time when her dreams were still undefined, but her determination was unmistakable. Like many young individuals, Emilie's early ambitions were born from a desire to carve out a future that was not limited by circumstances but shaped by the choices she made. As she entered her teenage years, she began to envision a life filled with possibilities, but it was only when she took her first active steps toward her goals that her path started to take shape.

The first significant step in Emilie's journey came during her high school years, when she recognized the power of education as a means to open doors to new opportunities. Despite the challenges that came with being a young woman in a society that sometimes imposed limitations on her, Emilie embraced the power of learning with a fervor that would set the tone for the rest of her life. Unlike many of her peers, who were more focused on socializing or following conventional paths, Emilie sought to excel academically and participate in activities that would push her outside her comfort zone.

Her high school years were marked by a thirst for knowledge that went beyond the classroom. Emilie joined various clubs and extracurricular activities, believing that these experiences would not only enrich her life but also help her build the skills necessary for future success. She became involved in leadership roles, particularly in debate clubs, where she honed her public speaking and critical thinking abilities. These early experiences taught Emilie how to communicate with clarity, engage in thoughtful discussions, and learn from diverse perspectives—a skillset that would later prove invaluable in her professional life.

Simultaneously, Emilie discovered a passion for social causes, which further fueled her desire to make a difference in the world. She volunteered for several community outreach programs, helping marginalized groups and contributing to local initiatives. Through these experiences, Emilie learned the importance of empathy, service, and the ability to create change at the grassroots level. These formative experiences shaped her worldview, giving her a sense of purpose and direction. She realized that her life's work would involve not only achieving personal success but also giving back to the community and helping others realize their own potential.

The next significant step in Emilie's journey came when she decided to pursue higher education. While many of her friends opted for traditional paths, Emilie set her sights on a university that would allow her to explore her intellectual curiosity and expand her skill set. She chose a field that she was deeply passionate about—one that would allow her to merge her interests in business, technology, and social impact. However, the decision to pursue a degree was not without its challenges. Emilie faced moments of self-doubt, particularly as she navigated the pressures of academia. The road ahead was often uncertain, and she questioned whether she was truly capable of succeeding in such a competitive environment. But with her mother's lessons of resilience and her father's emphasis on the value of perseverance, Emilie was determined to prove to herself and to others that she could rise above the odds.

During her time at university, Emilie took every opportunity to learn, grow, and apply herself. She sought internships, worked on projects that sparked her passion, and built a network of like-minded individuals who shared her aspirations. These early experiences were pivotal in helping Emilie refine her professional goals and develop the skills necessary to succeed in the real world. It was also during this time that Emilie began to realize the importance of mentorship. She actively sought guidance from professors, industry professionals, and peers who had experience in areas she was interested in. Their advice and mentorship helped her navigate the complexities of her chosen field and gave her the confidence to pursue her dreams further.

Emilie's first steps in her journey were not without obstacles. She faced the same challenges many young individuals face—balancing academics with personal life, dealing with moments of insecurity, and questioning her future. However, these hurdles only strengthened her resolve. Emilie understood that success was not a straight line but rather a series of twists and turns, each offering a new lesson. The more she encountered these obstacles, the more she grew, both personally and professionally.

The first steps in Emilie Kiser's journey set the foundation for everything that would follow. They were the beginning of a path that would lead her to challenge the expectations placed on her, pursue her dreams with determination, and ultimately make a lasting impact in her field. These early steps were filled with self-discovery, hard work, and ambition, marking the start of a remarkable journey that would shape Emilie into the person she would later become—a figure whose influence would extend far beyond her own expectations.

Key Moments that Shaped Her Path

For Emilie Kiser, success did not come easily, nor did it follow a straightforward path. Her journey was marked by a series of pivotal moments—each one a turning point that would shape her trajectory, refine her vision, and propel her toward the person she was destined to become. These moments, often born from unexpected circumstances, challenges, or encounters, played a critical role in not only defining her career but also in helping her grow as an individual.

One of the earliest key moments that profoundly shaped Emilie's path came during her time at university. As a young woman entering a competitive and sometimes intimidating environment, she quickly realized that academic excellence alone would not guarantee success. It was during her first major group project that Emilie experienced her first real leadership challenge. She had always been an effective individual contributor, but managing a team of diverse personalities was an entirely different skill set. The project quickly became tense as team members clashed over ideas, timelines, and responsibilities. In that moment, Emilie recognized the importance of not just intellectual capacity but emotional intelligence—the ability to listen, mediate, and build consensus within a group. Instead of leading through authority or frustration, Emilie learned how to navigate group dynamics with empathy and adaptability. The experience helped her understand that leadership is as much about people as it is about vision, and it marked the beginning of her development as a strategic thinker and leader.

Another moment that profoundly shaped Emilie came during her first internship. Fresh out of university and eager to gain real-world experience, she entered an organization with big expectations and high hopes. However, what she didn't anticipate was the sense of imposter syndrome that would soon grip her. Surrounded by seasoned professionals who seemed so much more capable and confident, Emilie initially struggled with feelings of inadequacy. Yet, instead of retreating, she chose to confront her insecurity head-on. She sought guidance from mentors within the company and asked for feedback, determined to improve her performance. In doing so, she not only grew her professional skillset but also developed the mental fortitude to navigate any future challenges. This internship was not just about learning the technical aspects of her field, but it also served as an awakening to the importance of resilience and continuous self-improvement.

A defining moment in Emilie's path came when she was offered a leadership role in a project that had been struggling to find direction. The project had fallen behind schedule, and morale was low. Many colleagues were skeptical of Emilie's ability to turn things around, given her relatively limited experience. However, she saw it as an opportunity to prove herself. Emilie took a step back, reassessed the situation, and redefined the project's goals, focusing on the bigger picture and aligning everyone's personal contributions with a shared vision. This shift in perspective inspired her team to work collaboratively, fostering a sense of ownership and accountability. Against the odds, Emilie managed to get the project back on track, demonstrating not only her ability to lead under pressure but also her capacity to inspire others. The success of this project solidified her reputation as a leader who could deliver results, even when the stakes were high.

Yet, perhaps one of the most transformative moments in Emilie's journey occurred during a particularly difficult personal setback. After a period of immense professional success, she experienced a personal loss that left her questioning her purpose and direction. For a time, Emilie struggled with balancing her emotions and her responsibilities, as she found herself in a place of profound vulnerability. However, this moment of adversity proved to be a crucible, forging a deeper understanding of herself and her true motivations. During this time, she began to reevaluate her priorities, focusing not just on external success but on finding a sense of internal peace and fulfillment. Emilie realized that her success was not solely defined by her achievements but by her ability to live authentically and with purpose. This reflection reshaped her career goals, and from that point on, she sought work that aligned with her values—work that not only allowed her to succeed but also gave her the opportunity to give back to the community and make a positive impact.

The culmination of these key moments—the leadership lessons, the overcoming of self-doubt, the personal reflection—created the foundation for Emilie's future. Each experience taught her that success is not just about reaching a destination but about navigating the journey with authenticity, resilience, and a sense of purpose. They shaped her into a woman who understood that every setback was an opportunity for growth and that every victory was the result of collaboration, reflection, and learning. These key moments helped Emilie Kiser become not just a professional success but a person who was grounded in her values and driven by the desire to create meaningful change in the world.

Chapter 2
The Breakthrough

Every journey toward success has its defining moments, and for Emilie Kiser, the breakthrough came when she least expected it. After years of hard work, perseverance, and overcoming countless hurdles, Emilie found herself at the crossroads of opportunity—a place where everything she had been working toward began to take shape. This chapter marks a pivotal moment in Emilie's life, the time when she transitioned from being an aspiring professional to a recognized figure in her field. It was a moment that not only validated her efforts but also propelled her into a new realm of possibility.

At the time, Emilie was navigating the early stages of her career, still learning the ropes and refining her skills. Although she had already achieved some early successes, the recognition she sought seemed distant. The work was often grueling, the competition fierce, and the path ahead uncertain. Despite this, Emilie remained focused, driven by the belief that her hard work would eventually pay off. She understood that success wasn't always immediate but rather a culmination of consistent effort, learning, and growth.

The breakthrough moment came unexpectedly, during a project that she had been working on for months. Initially, it seemed like just another task in a long line of assignments, something she needed to complete to move forward in her career. But as the project progressed, Emilie began to see the potential for something much bigger. The project, which involved collaborating with a team of professionals, required a fresh perspective, a combination of creativity and strategic thinking. Emilie, having honed her skills over time, saw an opportunity to take the project in a direction no one else had considered.

Her innovative approach and leadership skills caught the attention of her superiors, who recognized the potential impact her ideas could have on the company. What started as a routine assignment soon became the focal point of a larger initiative. Emilie's contributions elevated the project, and the success of her leadership turned the initiative into a company-wide success story. This marked the beginning of Emilie's breakthrough. It wasn't just the completion of a project—it was a moment of recognition, where her talent and potential were acknowledged on a larger scale.

But the breakthrough wasn't just about professional recognition; it was about Emilie finding her voice. For years, she had worked behind the scenes, doing the necessary work, honing her skills, and quietly pushing her way forward. Now, in the spotlight, Emilie realized that her ideas, her perspective, and her leadership mattered. She had earned her place at the table, not through luck but through relentless hard work and an unwavering belief in herself.

This moment of breakthrough also came with its own set of challenges. With recognition came responsibility, and Emilie soon realized that being in the spotlight meant facing higher expectations and greater scrutiny. The pressure to perform at an even higher level was overwhelming at times. But rather than shrinking from these challenges, Emilie embraced them, understanding that true growth happens when we step outside our comfort zones and rise to meet new challenges.

Emilie's breakthrough was not just a professional achievement; it was a personal transformation. It marked the moment when she fully embraced her role as a leader and visionary. The recognition she received reinforced the lessons she had learned earlier in her journey—the importance of resilience, the power of self-belief, and the value of collaboration. It was a reminder that the path to success is rarely linear, but with hard work, the right mindset, and a willingness to take risks, anything is possible.

As this chapter unfolds, we will explore the challenges Emilie faced during her breakthrough, the lessons she learned, and the new opportunities that arose from this pivotal moment. We will dive into the emotional, professional, and personal aspects of her transformation, shedding light on the process that led her to this life-changing moment. This breakthrough was not just a milestone in Emilie's career—it was the beginning of a new chapter, one that would propel her toward even greater heights and further solidify her place as a trailblazer in her field.

First Major Achievement

Every success story has a defining moment—a moment when everything changes and the dream transitions into reality. For Emilie Kiser, that moment arrived with her first major achievement, a milestone that not only validated her abilities but also cemented her place in her chosen field. This achievement, which came early in her career, marked the turning point where her hard work, skills, and aspirations collided to create something tangible. It was the moment when she realized that she had not only made it but had the ability to push boundaries, innovate, and lead.

Emilie's first major achievement came during a critical project early in her career, a project that many would have seen as just another routine assignment. However, for Emilie, it became an opportunity to demonstrate her true potential. When the project was first introduced, she was tasked with leading a team to develop a new marketing strategy for a product that had failed to meet expectations. The product, which had a great deal of potential, needed a fresh direction, and the company was looking for someone to turn things around. Emilie was given the responsibility, though with it came immense pressure. The stakes were high, and failure was not an option.

At first, Emilie was unsure of how to approach the challenge. The product's failure weighed heavily on the team, and morale was low. However, Emilie's ability to see beyond the obstacles and focus on solutions was what set her apart. She began by carefully analyzing the reasons for the product's lack of success and discovered several key areas for improvement. From there, Emilie set out to create a strategy that would not only address these issues but also breathe new life into the product. Her approach was innovative, blending traditional methods with modern, out-of-the-box thinking. Emilie brought a fresh perspective, combining her knowledge of market trends with a deep understanding of consumer behavior. She focused on reshaping the product's brand image, targeting a new audience, and enhancing its market presence through creative campaigns.

One of the key elements that made Emilie's strategy successful was her collaborative approach. Rather than working in isolation, she engaged her team at every stage of the process. She encouraged open communication, valued their input, and made sure everyone felt invested in the success of the project. Emilie's leadership not only motivated the team but also fostered a sense of ownership and pride in the work. By the end of the project, the team had produced a marketing campaign that was fresh, bold, and highly effective.

The results were nothing short of remarkable. Within a few months of the new campaign's launch, the product saw a significant increase in sales. The company was not only able to recover from the initial failure but also positioned the product as a strong contender in the market. Emilie's first major achievement had a tangible impact — both on her career and on the company's bottom line.

This achievement wasn't just about the numbers; it was about the way it transformed Emilie's professional identity. She had successfully led a project from start to finish, overcoming obstacles, managing a team, and delivering exceptional results. Her ability to turn a struggling product into a success proved that she had the skills to lead, innovate, and drive change. This accomplishment gave her the confidence to take on even greater challenges, and it marked the beginning of a series of successes that would define her career.

The recognition that followed was equally rewarding. Emilie's contribution was acknowledged by her superiors, and she was given increased responsibility and visibility within the company. Her achievement also attracted the attention of industry leaders, who began to see her as someone with the potential to lead at a higher level. This first major achievement served as a springboard, propelling her forward into more significant roles and projects.

However, what made this achievement truly significant was the personal growth that Emilie experienced. She realized that her success wasn't just about her technical skills or her ability to lead; it was about her ability to adapt, learn from failure, and remain resilient in the face of challenges. Emilie's first major achievement taught her that success is rarely linear and that the true measure of success lies in the lessons learned along the way.

Emilie's first major achievement was the catalyst for the incredible career that would follow. It was the moment when she proved to herself—and to others—that she had the potential to do great things. It set the stage for a future filled with even greater accomplishments, but most importantly, it marked a moment of self-realization. Emilie had not only proved her capabilities but had also set the foundation for the future she envisioned—one built on hard work, creativity, and the courage to take risks.

Recognition and Media Attention

As Emilie Kiser's career began to gain momentum, the recognition and media attention she received played a pivotal role in shaping her professional journey and solidifying her place in her field. What began as a series of small but significant achievements eventually caught the attention of industry leaders, influencers, and media outlets, catapulting her into the public eye. However, the recognition was not just about the accolades; it was about the opportunities and responsibilities that came with it, as well as the challenges of navigating fame while staying true to her values and goals.

It all started with Emilie's first major achievement, which caught the attention of her superiors and colleagues alike. Her success with the marketing campaign and product revival had a ripple effect. The company leadership was impressed by her innovative approach and her ability to lead a team under pressure. Soon, word of her success spread within the company, and Emilie's name became synonymous with both creativity and results. But it wasn't just the internal recognition that mattered—it was also the external acknowledgment that followed. The media took note of the success story, and soon

Emilie found herself being featured in industry publications and interviewed by media outlets eager to share her journey.

The recognition came in various forms, from feature articles in well-regarded business magazines to interviews on popular podcasts. Emilie's story resonated with audiences because it wasn't just about her professional success—it was about the obstacles she overcame, the perseverance she demonstrated, and the way she defied expectations. She became a symbol of resilience and innovation, and her story became a source of inspiration for many young professionals, especially women, aspiring to break into competitive industries.

With media attention came a broader platform, and Emilie was faced with new challenges. As her visibility grew, so did the scrutiny. She had to learn how to balance her newfound fame with her desire for privacy. The media often painted her in a polished, idealized light, but Emilie was mindful of the fact that success was not always glamorous. Behind every public success were countless hours of hard work, mistakes, and moments of doubt. She wanted to maintain an authentic presence, one that reflected both the highs and lows of her journey.

One of the key aspects of Emilie's media presence was her ability to stay grounded despite the growing attention. She remained focused on her work and kept her values front and center. Emilie knew that the media spotlight, while flattering, could sometimes distract from the true essence of her achievements. She worked hard to keep her narrative clear and true to her own experiences, rather than allowing external pressures to define her. She became known not just for her accomplishments but for her authenticity in the face of a world that often glorified perfection.

Despite the pressure, Emilie understood the power of media exposure and used it to further her professional goals. She became an advocate for causes close to her heart, using her platform to speak about diversity, gender equality, and the importance of mentorship. Her media appearances often focused on these issues, and Emilie quickly gained a reputation not just as a successful professional, but as a role model who was using her position to bring about change. Through interviews, panel discussions, and keynote speeches, Emilie advocated for the next generation of leaders and worked to amplify voices that had historically been underrepresented.

The recognition and media attention also opened doors to new opportunities. Emilie began receiving offers to collaborate with other professionals and brands that aligned with her values. She was invited to speak at conferences, lead workshops, and participate in initiatives that supported social causes and innovation. Each opportunity further enhanced her reputation, and Emilie carefully selected those that allowed her to continue growing while contributing meaningfully to her industry.

However, the increased recognition did come with its challenges. As Emilie's profile grew, so did the expectations placed on her. She was now seen not just as a talented individual but as a representative of her industry. The pressure to constantly perform, to always have the right answers, and to maintain a certain level of public engagement was immense. Emilie learned to manage these expectations by setting clear boundaries and staying focused on her long-term goals. She relied on her network of mentors and peers for support and guidance, recognizing that success was not a solitary pursuit but one that required collaboration and a solid foundation of relationships.

Emilie's rise to prominence through recognition and media attention was a crucial chapter in her journey. It marked the moment when her hard work and vision were acknowledged on a larger scale, opening doors to new opportunities and platforms. But it also marked the beginning of a new set of challenges—one that required balance, authenticity, and a commitment to staying true to her mission. Despite the complexities of navigating public life, Emilie Kiser emerged stronger, more focused, and even more determined to make a lasting impact in her field and beyond. The media attention that had once seemed like a distant dream was now a tool she wielded carefully, using her voice to inspire others and create meaningful change.

Challenges Faced Along the Way

No journey toward success is without its hurdles, and Emilie Kiser's path to prominence was no exception. Along the way, she encountered a series of challenges that tested her resolve, forced her to evolve, and ultimately shaped the person she would become. While many of these challenges seemed insurmountable at times, they became the stepping stones that propelled her forward, refining her skills, and reinforcing her belief in her ability to succeed despite adversity. These struggles, both internal and external, played an integral role in shaping Emilie's character and her approach to leadership.

One of the first major challenges Emilie faced was dealing with the overwhelming pressure to prove herself. Early in her career, she was often the youngest person in the room, tasked with leading teams and making decisions that impacted large-scale projects. As a result, she often felt the weight of needing to demonstrate not just competence, but exceptional capability in everything she did. The expectation to be perfect weighed heavily on her, and it became clear that the demands of leadership came with constant scrutiny. For a while, Emilie struggled with imposter syndrome—the feeling that she didn't truly belong in the positions she had earned. She questioned whether her achievements were a result of her own talent or simply luck.

Despite her doubts, Emilie learned to navigate this challenge by embracing vulnerability and seeking feedback from mentors and peers. Rather than letting her insecurities hold her back, she leaned into her discomfort, using it as a driving force to continuously improve. She recognized that the need for validation would never go away, but the more she focused on learning from her mistakes and growing, the less she relied on external approval. This internal shift helped her develop the mental strength to face challenges with confidence.

Another significant challenge came from navigating the complexities of the workplace culture, particularly as a woman in a male-dominated industry. Emilie often found herself in environments where her ideas were initially dismissed or undervalued simply because of her gender. She encountered situations where her male colleagues were given credit for ideas she had presented or where her contributions were minimized. At times, this bias was subtle, but it was nonetheless pervasive, and it caused Emilie to question her own worth in the workplace.

Rather than shrinking back, Emilie chose to confront these challenges head-on. She became an advocate for herself and for other women in the industry, speaking out when necessary and ensuring that her voice was heard. She learned to assert herself more confidently in meetings, taking ownership of her ideas and ensuring that they were credited to her. Emilie's determination to fight against these biases not only helped her grow professionally but also led her to become an advocate for gender equality and diversity in the workplace. Over time, she built a network of allies who supported her and helped her navigate the challenges of being a woman in a competitive industry.

The pressure of maintaining a high level of performance also took a personal toll on Emilie. As her career progressed and her success became more public, she found herself stretched thin, juggling the demands of work with her personal life. The constant need to perform at a high level left little room for rest, and she often found herself overwhelmed. Emilie was determined to prove herself in every aspect of her life, but she soon realized that something had to give. The intense work schedule, combined with the pressure to succeed in a highly visible role, began to impact her mental and physical well-being.

After struggling with burnout and exhaustion, Emilie came to a crucial realization: no amount of success was worth sacrificing her health or happiness. She sought balance by learning how to delegate more effectively, setting boundaries with her time, and prioritizing self-care. This challenge, though difficult, taught her the importance of mental and physical well-being in sustaining long-term success. She also began to advocate for a healthier work-life balance, using her platform to encourage others in her industry to do the same.

Perhaps one of the most challenging experiences for Emilie was dealing with personal setbacks that affected her professional life. During a pivotal moment in her career, she experienced a personal loss that left her feeling emotionally and mentally drained. The grief and emotional turmoil she faced were hard to reconcile with her public persona and her professional obligations. There were moments when Emilie questioned whether she could continue at the pace she had set or if she needed to step back and focus on her personal healing.

However, this personal challenge became one of the defining moments of Emilie's journey. It was through this period of grief that Emilie learned to lean into vulnerability and accepted that it was okay to not be okay. She took time to heal, but she also allowed herself the space to mourn and grow. During this time, she developed a deeper sense of empathy for others and a more profound understanding of the importance of emotional resilience. When she returned to work, Emilie did so with a renewed sense of purpose, recognizing that her personal experiences had made her not only a stronger leader but also a more compassionate and understanding individual.

The challenges Emilie Kiser faced along the way were undeniably difficult, but they were essential to her growth and success. They taught her valuable lessons in resilience, self-advocacy, balance, and emotional strength. Rather than being obstacles, these challenges became opportunities for Emilie to define her own path, develop her leadership skills, and emerge stronger and more capable. Through it all, Emilie learned that the road to success is not linear, and it is the ability to navigate the bumps along the way that ultimately leads to fulfillment and achievement.

The Turning Point in Her Career

Every career has a turning point—the moment when everything aligns, and the trajectory shifts toward a new level of success and influence. For Emilie Kiser, this turning point came at a time when she had already proven herself capable and hardworking but was still searching for the true opportunity to showcase her full potential.

After years of navigating challenges and gaining valuable experience, Emilie's breakthrough moment arrived in a way that she never expected. It was the moment when she realized that she had the ability to shape her own future, take risks, and create something truly transformative in her field.

The turning point occurred when Emilie was offered the opportunity to lead a high-profile project within her company—one that had the potential to redefine the business landscape. The project was to launch a new product line aimed at a niche market that had been largely underserved. While the concept was intriguing, the product itself faced numerous hurdles, including market skepticism and the challenge of building brand credibility from scratch. This was not just another project; it was an opportunity that could make or break her career.

When Emilie first received the assignment, she was both excited and overwhelmed. The expectations were high, and the pressure to succeed was immense. It was not just about delivering results; it was about proving her ability to lead at the highest level. Despite her growing reputation for success, the thought of managing such a complex and high-stakes initiative left her feeling both exhilarated and uncertain. But Emilie understood the magnitude of the opportunity in front of her. This project was her chance to step into a leadership role that was far beyond anything she had experienced before.

Emilie approached the project with the same dedication and passion that had marked every previous task. However, this time, she took a different approach. She saw the project not just as a means to prove her worth but as an opportunity to push boundaries and redefine what was possible. Emilie took the time to thoroughly understand the market, the product's potential, and the needs of the audience. Instead of relying solely on traditional strategies, she began to incorporate innovative methods, blending creativity with strategic thinking. She assembled a team of experts who could contribute to the various aspects of the project and ensured that every voice was heard, fostering a sense of ownership and commitment within the team.

The turning point truly came when Emilie's vision for the project began to take shape. Her strategic thinking, combined with her ability to rally her team and inspire them, led to a series of successful initiatives that transformed the product from a concept into a marketable force. Emilie's approach was groundbreaking—she didn't simply rely on conventional marketing tactics; she pushed the envelope by leveraging digital platforms, social media, and influencer partnerships that resonated with the target audience. The product was positioned not just as a commodity, but as a lifestyle choice, creating an emotional connection with consumers.

The launch of the product line exceeded expectations. The brand became an instant success, rapidly gaining traction in the market and earning recognition from both industry insiders and the media. Sales exceeded projections, and the product quickly became a symbol of innovation and leadership in the industry. Emilie's strategic brilliance had paid off, but it was not just the financial success that marked the turning point in her career—it was the recognition of her leadership and vision.

What made this turning point so significant was not just the successful completion of the project, but the transformation it represented for Emilie. It was the moment when she realized that her career could no longer be defined by just her hard work and ability to execute tasks. This project proved to her that she could create something that was uniquely her own, that she could lead with vision and purpose, and that she had the power to influence the direction of her industry. She had proven that she was not just a capable manager, but a forward-thinking leader who could innovate and inspire.

The success of this project propelled Emilie into the spotlight, and she was soon recognized as one of the leading figures in her field. Invitations to speak at industry conferences, participate in high-profile panels, and collaborate with influential figures began to pour in. The company, impressed by her accomplishments, offered her even more prominent roles, and Emilie's professional network expanded exponentially. But perhaps the most important change was within herself. This turning point solidified her confidence in her ability to lead at the highest levels, and it marked the beginning of a new chapter in her career—a chapter defined by ambition, influence, and the courage to embrace challenges.

The turning point in Emilie Kiser's career was not just a professional achievement—it was a personal awakening. It was the moment when she stopped seeing herself as someone working her way up the ladder and began to see herself as someone capable of shaping her own path and impacting her field on a larger scale. This moment marked the beginning of her true leadership journey, one that would continue to evolve and inspire others as she took on greater challenges and achieved even greater successes.

Chapter 3
The Rise to Prominence

After the turning point in her career, when Emilie Kiser proved her ability to lead and innovate, the trajectory of her professional life changed forever. This chapter marks the period when Emilie transitioned from being a successful up-and-comer to a recognized force in her industry. Her rise to prominence was not the result of a single achievement but a culmination of her leadership, vision, and relentless pursuit of excellence. It was a time when the foundation she had laid through years of hard work and dedication finally began to bear fruit, and Emilie found herself at the center of major industry conversations.

The rise to prominence was not without its challenges, though. As Emilie's success grew, so did the visibility of her work. She found herself in situations where her decisions and strategies were under constant scrutiny, and expectations were higher than ever before. With greater recognition came greater responsibility, and Emilie quickly realized that her actions and choices would be scrutinized by not just her team but the industry at large. The pressure to maintain her success was immense, but instead of succumbing to the weight of these expectations, Emilie embraced them as an opportunity to further elevate her work and influence.

One of the key factors that contributed to Emilie's rise was her ability to consistently innovate. Her work wasn't just about doing things well; it was about doing things differently. Emilie's ideas, her ability to think outside the box, and her willingness to take calculated risks set her apart from others in her field. Her willingness to challenge the status quo and push boundaries allowed her to create solutions and strategies that hadn't been seen before. Emilie understood that true leadership meant not just following trends but creating them. It was this forward-thinking approach that propelled her into the spotlight and made her an influential figure in her industry.

Another important aspect of Emilie's rise was her strategic use of networking and mentorship. Throughout her career, she had been intentional about building relationships with industry leaders, influencers, and mentors who shared her values and could offer guidance. These relationships played a crucial role in opening doors for Emilie, allowing her to gain access to opportunities that would have otherwise been out of reach. Whether it was through speaking engagements, collaborations, or partnerships, Emilie's network of supporters helped amplify her voice and gave her the platform to showcase her talents on a larger scale.

Additionally, Emilie's personal brand began to take shape during this time. She understood the importance of creating a cohesive and authentic narrative around her work and her values. She wasn't just another professional in her field—she was a thought leader, an innovator, and an advocate for positive change. Emilie used her platform to speak out on important issues, including gender equality, workplace diversity, and the importance of mentorship. Her ability to balance her career with advocacy efforts helped solidify her as a well-rounded leader, someone who was committed to making a difference not just through her professional accomplishments but through her broader societal contributions.

As Emilie's profile grew, so did the opportunities that came her way. Major companies and organizations sought her expertise, and she was offered leadership roles that expanded her influence even further. Whether it was heading global initiatives, consulting for industry giants, or becoming a sought-after speaker at conferences, Emilie found herself being invited to the table in spaces where her voice mattered. With every opportunity, she continued to rise, solidifying her place as one of the leading figures in her industry.

However, the rise to prominence was not without its sacrifices. As Emilie's career reached new heights, she found herself grappling with the challenges of maintaining balance. The demands of her professional life often encroached on her personal time, and the pressure to stay at the top was constant. Emilie had to learn how to manage this new phase of her career, ensuring that she continued to prioritize her health, relationships, and personal well-being while pursuing her professional goals.

The rise to prominence was not just about career achievements; it was about the evolution of Emilie as a leader, a role model, and a change-maker. It was during this time that Emilie fully embraced her role as a thought leader and began to have a lasting impact on the industry she loved. She became a source of inspiration for others, especially young women looking to break into competitive industries, and her story served as a testament to the power of hard work, resilience, and staying true to one's values.

In this chapter, we will explore the events, decisions, and challenges that contributed to Emilie Kiser's rise to prominence. From her innovative approach to leadership to her ability to navigate the pressures of success, this period of Emilie's career laid the groundwork for the powerful influence she would continue to wield.

It was a time of growth, recognition, and transformation—both professionally and personally—and it marked the beginning of a new era in Emilie's career, one where she would not only achieve greatness but also inspire others to follow in her footsteps.

Gaining National Attention

As Emilie Kiser's career progressed, the seeds she had sown through years of hard work, strategic thinking, and relentless pursuit of excellence began to bloom in the form of national recognition. What started as a series of successful projects, innovative ideas, and leadership accomplishments soon garnered attention on a much larger scale. Emilie found herself thrust into the public eye, as her work began to resonate not only within her industry but also with the broader national audience. The moment she gained national attention was both a validation of her efforts and a challenge to maintain the high standards she had set for herself.

The initial breakthrough in national recognition came when Emilie's innovative work on a high-profile project was picked up by industry publications. Her ability to turn a failing product into a major success through a mix of creative marketing strategies and leadership was lauded as an example of how businesses could reinvent themselves. National business outlets began to take notice of her expertise in navigating challenges and leading teams to success. Feature articles, interviews, and case studies soon followed, and Emilie's name became synonymous with innovation, leadership, and success. It was not just the outcome of the project that drew attention, but the unique approach she took in rethinking the strategy and leading her team through uncharted waters.

As her profile grew within the business community, Emilie was invited to speak at national conferences, where her insights into leadership, innovation, and workplace diversity were in high demand. These speaking engagements marked the beginning of her influence beyond her immediate professional circle. Emilie shared her story of overcoming obstacles, embracing new perspectives, and leading with authenticity, and her message resonated with audiences across various industries. People began to see Emilie not only as a successful businesswoman but as a thought leader capable of shaping the future of her field. Her talks, filled with both inspiration and practical advice, began to attract large audiences, and soon she was seen as a role model for aspiring professionals, particularly women looking to break into leadership roles in male-dominated industries.

The media attention that followed her speaking engagements and written features allowed Emilie to influence public conversations about leadership, innovation, and the importance of diversity in the workplace. National publications began to seek her expertise on current trends, and she was often called upon for her opinion on industry matters. Emilie's ability to articulate complex ideas in a relatable and impactful way made her a sought-after commentator and contributor to thought leadership discussions. Her perspectives on the need for a more inclusive workforce, the power of mentorship, and the evolving nature of leadership became a central part of her public identity.

However, gaining national attention also brought new challenges. Emilie now found herself balancing the demands of her growing public profile with the responsibilities of her professional work. The pressure to maintain a positive image, remain relevant, and continually deliver results became overwhelming at times. She was no longer just an expert in her field—she was a public figure, and her every move was under scrutiny. This shift required Emilie to develop new skills in managing her public persona while staying grounded in her values and goals. She had to learn how to navigate the delicate balance between being a role model and staying true to her authentic self.

Despite these pressures, Emilie remained committed to using her newfound visibility for positive change. She recognized that national attention was an opportunity to advocate for causes she believed in. She became increasingly vocal about the importance of diversity, women's empowerment, and the need for greater representation in leadership positions. Emilie used her platform to speak out about gender inequality in the workplace, the challenges faced by women of color, and the necessity of creating spaces where all voices could be heard. Her advocacy work expanded beyond her professional sphere, as she partnered with organizations to mentor young women and minorities seeking careers in business and leadership.

Gaining national attention also brought more responsibility, but Emilie was up to the challenge. She continued to take on high-profile projects, each one more challenging than the last, and leveraged her platform to foster change in her industry. She became a trusted advisor to top companies and a sought-after speaker at conferences and panels, where her opinions were respected by peers and competitors alike. Through her work and her public presence, Emilie demonstrated that true leadership goes beyond achieving success—it involves using one's platform to advocate for meaningful change and inspire others to pursue their dreams.

Ultimately, gaining national attention marked a turning point in Emilie's career. It was the moment when her expertise, leadership, and vision were recognized on a broader scale. More than just a personal achievement, this recognition allowed Emilie to influence the direction of her industry and contribute to shaping the future of business and leadership. It solidified her place as a trailblazer and thought leader, but it also reinforced her commitment to using her success as a vehicle for creating a more inclusive and diverse world. Through her rise to national prominence, Emilie Kiser became a symbol of what is possible when talent, resilience, and advocacy intersect in meaningful ways.

Career Milestones and Achievements

Emilie Kiser's career is marked by a series of milestones and achievements that demonstrate not only her professional capabilities but also her unwavering dedication to excellence, innovation, and leadership. Each milestone represents a significant step forward, a testament to her ability to overcome challenges, take calculated risks, and continuously evolve in a competitive industry. From her early accomplishments to her rise as a thought leader in her field, Emilie's journey is a narrative of relentless ambition, strategic decision-making, and transformative contributions that have left a lasting impact on both her career and the industry at large.

One of the first major milestones in Emilie's career came when she successfully led a turnaround project that saved a failing product line. The challenge was significant: the product had not met sales expectations, and the team was unsure how to reintroduce it to the market. As the lead strategist, Emilie took charge of the situation with a combination of market analysis, creative thinking, and bold decision-making. She initiated a complete overhaul of the product's branding, positioning, and marketing strategy, targeting a new demographic and leveraging digital platforms to create buzz. The campaign's success not only revived the product but also helped establish Emilie's reputation as someone capable of transforming struggling projects into profitable ventures. This achievement solidified her role as a trusted leader within her company and set the stage for future opportunities.

Building on this success, Emilie continued to climb the ranks within her organization. One of the defining moments in her career came when she was promoted to a senior leadership role, where she was entrusted with overseeing a large-scale initiative to expand the company's global presence. This milestone marked a shift in Emilie's career from a project manager to a strategic leader, responsible for high-level decisions that would impact the company's direction. The global expansion project was an ambitious undertaking, requiring coordination across multiple teams, markets, and regions. Emilie's ability to navigate the complexities of international markets, manage cross-cultural teams, and implement strategies that aligned with the company's vision led to a successful expansion. The initiative not only increased the company's revenue but also positioned Emilie as a key driver of its future growth.

As Emilie's career progressed, she became increasingly known for her expertise in leadership and innovation, and her achievements began to garner attention outside of her company. She was invited to speak at industry conferences and share her insights on topics such as leadership, business strategy, and the importance of diversity in the workplace. Her first major public speaking engagement was a defining moment, showcasing her ability to engage and inspire large audiences. Over time, Emilie became a sought-after speaker, invited to present at conferences, webinars, and panel discussions on a variety of business-related topics. Her ability to communicate complex ideas with clarity and passion helped her build a personal brand as a thought leader and influencer.

Another significant milestone in Emilie's career came when she was recognized by a prestigious business publication as one of the "Top 40 Under 40" in her industry. This accolade was a reflection of not only her professional achievements but also her impact on the business world. The recognition helped elevate Emilie's profile, opening doors to new opportunities and collaborations with some of the most respected names in her field. It was a clear indication that her work was being acknowledged on a broader scale, and it further motivated her to continue striving for excellence.

In addition to her work in business strategy and leadership, Emilie also began to focus on giving back to the community and empowering others. One of the most meaningful milestones in her career was the launch of a mentorship program designed to help young women break into leadership roles. Emilie had always been passionate about the importance of mentorship, and she recognized that providing guidance to the next generation of leaders was a powerful way to create lasting change. Through the program, Emilie mentored numerous young professionals, sharing her experiences, offering career advice, and helping them navigate the complexities of leadership. The success of the mentorship program became a major source of fulfillment for Emilie, as it allowed her to make a tangible difference in the lives of others.

One of the most rewarding achievements for Emilie came when she successfully transitioned into entrepreneurship. After years of leading large-scale initiatives and making a significant impact in her industry, Emilie decided to launch her own consulting firm, focusing on leadership development, business strategy, and diversity and inclusion. The decision to venture out on her own was both exciting and challenging, but Emilie's extensive experience, strong network, and passion for helping others succeed set her up for success. Her consulting firm quickly gained traction, working with clients across various industries to help them implement innovative strategies, build diverse teams, and create sustainable growth.

Emilie's career milestones and achievements are not just a reflection of her professional success but also a testament to her character, resilience, and commitment to making a positive impact. Each milestone represents a moment in time when Emilie stepped up, faced challenges head-on, and emerged stronger, more capable, and more determined to leave a lasting legacy. From turning around a struggling product line to launching her own business, Emilie Kiser's achievements demonstrate the power of vision, leadership, and a relentless pursuit of excellence. Through her career, she has proven that success is not defined by the accolades or titles one holds but by the difference one makes in the world.

Navigating Fame and Public Scrutiny

As Emilie Kiser's career progressed, the increasing recognition she garnered eventually brought with it a new set of challenges—fame and public scrutiny. While the acknowledgment of her achievements and growing influence were gratifying, the public spotlight cast a shadow that she had to navigate carefully. For someone who had spent years focused on her work and honing her skills, stepping into the public eye meant facing an entirely different set of expectations, pressures, and sometimes, criticisms. Emilie's ability to manage fame and public scrutiny would define her not only as a leader but also as a person of resilience, authenticity, and grace.

Initially, Emilie found the attention flattering. When she first started receiving recognition for her contributions to her industry, it felt like the culmination of all her hard work. Media features, interviews, and speaking engagements came one after another, and

Emilie was both honored and excited to share her story. But with every new appearance and accolade came a growing sense of responsibility, as her public persona began to take on a life of its own. She was no longer just Emilie the professional—she was becoming a public figure, and that shift was a transition that required her to rethink how she approached her career and personal life.

One of the first challenges Emilie faced was the pressure to always appear "perfect." In a world where social media highlights the curated best of people's lives, Emilie was expected to maintain a flawless image. Her achievements, the way she dressed, the way she spoke—everything was under the public microscope. People no longer just admired her for her professional abilities but began to judge her for her appearance, her demeanor, and even her personal decisions. The pressure to maintain an idealized image was overwhelming, and it created a sense of vulnerability that Emilie had never experienced before. The constant scrutiny, whether from the media or the public, left her feeling exposed, as though her every move was being watched and judged.

For Emilie, one of the hardest aspects of this fame was dealing with negative criticism. No matter how hard she worked or how much she achieved, there were always detractors. Negative comments, online trolling, and public disparagement came with the territory of being a prominent figure, especially one who was pushing boundaries in a traditionally male-dominated industry. The critiques were often harsh, focusing not on her ideas or leadership but on her personal life, appearance, or gender. Emilie initially struggled with these comments, taking them personally and allowing them to affect her confidence. But over time, she came to understand that criticism, while difficult, was an inevitable part of being in the public eye. Instead of internalizing the negativity, she began to view it as an opportunity to grow, learn, and focus even more on the impact she wanted to create.

One of Emilie's most significant realizations during this period was that authenticity would be her greatest asset. She understood that no matter how much she tried to fit into the mold of what the public expected her to be, she could never please everyone. Instead of conforming to the expectations of perfection, Emilie chose to remain true to herself. She shared the highs and the lows of her journey—her successes as well as her struggles. She became open about the challenges she faced, whether they were personal or professional, and used her platform to have honest conversations about the realities of leadership, gender dynamics, and the pursuit of success. By doing so, she broke down the walls of perfection that often surrounded successful women in the public eye and offered a more relatable and human version of herself.

Emilie also learned how to create boundaries. In the early stages of her fame, she felt compelled to accept every interview request, every speaking engagement, and every opportunity that came her way. However, over time, the relentless demand on her time and energy started to take a toll. She realized that to maintain her mental and emotional health, she needed to prioritize her well-being and set boundaries around her work and personal life. This meant learning to say "no" to opportunities that did not align with her values or her long-term goals. By establishing these boundaries, Emilie was able to preserve the integrity of her work while maintaining a sense of balance and peace in her personal life.

Despite the challenges, Emilie also recognized the immense power that fame and public scrutiny afforded her. With her increased visibility, she had the platform to advocate for causes she believed in—especially issues related to diversity, inclusion, and gender equality. She used her voice to speak out against workplace discrimination, promote equal opportunities for women in leadership, and encourage others to pursue their passions regardless of the obstacles they faced. This sense of purpose allowed Emilie to navigate fame with greater clarity, as she focused on the bigger picture and the positive impact she could make in the world.

Ultimately, Emilie Kiser's ability to navigate fame and public scrutiny transformed her from a successful professional to an influential leader and role model. She didn't allow the pressures of public life to derail her ambitions; instead, she used them as a platform for growth, advocacy, and continued success. By staying true to her authentic self and creating healthy boundaries, Emilie not only weathered the challenges of fame but also grew stronger and more resilient as a result.

The Support System Behind Her Success

While Emilie Kiser's name may be the one recognized in the spotlight, her success is far from a solo achievement. Behind every significant milestone and career triumph, there has been a strong and steadfast support system that has helped her navigate challenges, celebrate wins, and stay grounded in the face of overwhelming expectations. Emilie's journey to prominence is a testament not just to her personal drive and determination, but also to the importance of surrounding oneself with the right people—mentors, colleagues, friends, and family—who provide encouragement, guidance, and strength when needed most.

One of the cornerstones of Emilie's support system has always been her family. From a young age, Emilie's parents instilled in her the values of hard work, perseverance, and integrity. They taught her that success was not defined by accolades alone but by the character you built along the way. Her mother, in particular, was a pivotal influence, demonstrating what it meant to balance professional ambition with personal fulfillment. She was an unwavering role model for Emilie, showing her how to navigate the complexities of being a working professional and a mother, all while maintaining compassion and grace. Emilie's father, on the other hand, provided a steady foundation of wisdom and emotional support. His calm demeanor and belief in Emilie's potential helped her develop the confidence to push through difficult times and take bold risks.

Beyond her parents, Emilie's siblings have also been a source of constant support. Growing up in a tight-knit family, she found herself surrounded by people who not only cheered for her but also provided honest feedback when necessary. This familial bond, built on mutual respect and trust, has been a source of strength for Emilie, particularly during the times when she doubted herself or faced setbacks. Her siblings have always been her safe space—a reminder that success is not just about individual accomplishment, but about lifting one another up along the way.

As Emilie's career evolved and she moved into leadership roles, the importance of professional mentors and advisors became even more apparent. One of the most crucial aspects of Emilie's success has been her ability to seek guidance from individuals who have more experience and expertise in areas where she might be less knowledgeable. From early on, she surrounded herself with mentors who could offer valuable insights into leadership, business strategy, and navigating the complexities of corporate environments. These mentors not only helped Emilie grow professionally but also acted as sounding boards when she faced critical decisions. Whether it was advice on managing a high-stakes project or guidance on balancing the pressures of public scrutiny, Emilie's mentors played an integral role in her development as a leader.

Additionally, Emilie built a strong network of colleagues and peers who shared her vision and values. In the fast-paced world she navigated, having a trusted team of professionals to collaborate with was indispensable. Emilie fostered relationships with people who were not only skilled in their respective fields but also deeply committed to mutual success. Her colleagues were vital to her ability to innovate and take on larger, more complex projects. Whether it was a group of marketing experts working on a new campaign or a team of strategists collaborating on a new product launch, Emilie understood that no great achievement was ever the result of a single individual. Her ability to build strong, cohesive teams allowed her to leverage collective wisdom and work toward shared goals.

Perhaps one of the most significant sources of support for Emilie came from her close circle of friends. In an industry where competition can often feel fierce, Emilie found herself fortunate to have friends who weren't just colleagues but genuine companions. These friendships provided her with emotional support and a space to recharge. When the pressures of her career became overwhelming, her friends offered not just advice but also empathy, reminding her of the importance of self-care, mental health, and perspective. These friendships allowed Emilie to stay balanced and reminded her that success wasn't just about the external accolades, but about the joy of authentic connections and shared experiences.

In times of personal struggle or professional burnout, Emilie's support system helped her navigate difficult moments with grace and resilience. She knew that to continue her upward trajectory, she needed to not only rely on her own strength but also lean on those who had always been there for her. The guidance and encouragement she received from her support system—whether through tough conversations, quiet moments of reassurance, or bursts of shared celebration—provided Emilie with the tools and mindset needed to keep moving forward.

The support system behind Emilie Kiser's success is a blend of family, mentors, colleagues, and friends who have all contributed to her growth in unique and invaluable ways. While Emilie's name may be the one etched on the achievements, it is the collective effort of those around her that has empowered her to achieve greatness. By surrounding herself with people who inspire, challenge, and uplift her, Emilie has been able to not only realize her professional goals but also remain grounded in the values that have guided her from the beginning. Through their unwavering support, Emilie has been able to rise to prominence and continue her journey toward making a lasting impact in her field.

Chapter 4
Personal Struggles and Resilience

Success is often portrayed as a seamless progression—one achievement following another, each success building upon the last. However, the reality behind most successful individuals is far more complex. For Emilie Kiser, her journey to prominence was not without significant personal struggles. The external recognition and professional triumphs she earned were the result of not only hard work and determination but also the resilience she developed in the face of adversity. This chapter delves into the personal struggles Emilie faced—challenges that tested her emotionally, mentally, and physically—and explores how these struggles shaped her into the leader and individual she would ultimately become.

From the outset of her career, Emilie faced an ongoing balancing act between her professional and personal life. As her career began to flourish, the demands of work often clashed with her need for rest and personal time. She was a perfectionist by nature, always striving for excellence in every aspect of her life, whether at work or at home. But the relentless pace of her professional life left little room for self-care, and Emilie found herself stretched thin. The pressure to perform at the highest level in both her career and personal life led to a sense of burnout, something she had not anticipated despite all her careful planning. It became clear that she was pushing herself to the brink, trying to meet the expectations she had set for herself without acknowledging her own limitations.

As the pressure mounted, Emilie struggled with feelings of guilt. She felt that she wasn't giving enough of herself to her family, her friends, or her own well-being. She began to question whether it was possible to achieve success without sacrificing the things she held dear. Her work-life balance was at a breaking point, and it was in these moments of reflection that Emilie began to confront the reality that her relentless pursuit of perfection was unsustainable. This personal struggle forced her to reevaluate her priorities and reframe her definition of success. The idea of being "everything to everyone" was a myth, and Emilie needed to redefine her approach to both work and life in order to find harmony between the two.

On top of professional burnout, Emilie also faced significant personal loss during this time. The death of a close family member hit her hard, leaving her emotionally devastated. The loss was not only a personal blow but also a reminder of the fragility of life. Emilie struggled with grief and loss, and for the first time in years, she found herself questioning everything. How could she continue to push forward in her career when she was so deeply affected by the personal turmoil she was experiencing? These emotional struggles were compounded by the pressure to maintain her public persona, and for a time, Emilie felt disconnected from both her professional life and her personal sense of self.

Yet, despite these immense challenges, Emilie's resilience began to shine through. Rather than allowing the personal hardships to derail her, she confronted them head-on, learning to process her grief, embrace her vulnerability, and lean into her support system. She realized that the struggle was not a sign of weakness, but a natural part of the human experience. Emilie sought therapy and guidance, and slowly, she began to regain her sense of balance and perspective. The experience forced her to let go of the perfectionism that had once driven her and embrace a new understanding of success—one that included both achievement and self-compassion.

Emilie's personal struggles taught her the invaluable lesson of resilience—not just bouncing back from adversity but growing stronger because of it. She learned to redefine what it meant to be "successful," recognizing that true success was not about flawless achievement, but about how one faced challenges and emerged from them with newfound strength. Emilie's ability to process grief, confront her weaknesses, and maintain her drive in the face of personal difficulty became a cornerstone of her character. Through her struggles, she discovered the depth of her own resilience—a resilience that would continue to serve her throughout her career and personal life.

This chapter explores how Emilie's personal struggles played an essential role in shaping the woman she would become. From balancing the pressures of career and family to navigating the loss of a loved one, Emilie's journey is one of profound self-discovery and strength. Her struggles were not roadblocks but rather stepping stones that helped her build the resilience necessary to thrive in both her personal and professional life. Through each challenge, Emilie learned that success is not about perfection; it is about embracing adversity, finding strength in vulnerability, and continuing to move forward, no matter how difficult the path may seem.

Behind the Scenes: Personal Challenges

Behind every professional achievement, there often lies a set of personal challenges that are not seen by the public eye. For Emilie

Kiser, her rise to prominence came with not only the external pressures of maintaining success but also personal struggles that tested her emotional resilience, mental strength, and sense of self. While the world saw the polished image of a successful leader, the reality was much more complex. This chapter explores the personal challenges Emilie faced behind the scenes—challenges that shaped her into the person she is today, as well as the lessons she learned from overcoming them.

One of the most significant personal challenges Emilie dealt with was managing the expectations of both herself and others. As she gained recognition in her field, the pressure to constantly perform at a high level became overwhelming. She had always held herself to the highest standards, but as her career progressed, the demands from her professional life grew exponentially. The constant drive for perfection in her work often led Emilie to push herself beyond healthy limits, sacrificing her mental and physical well-being in pursuit of achievement. She found herself caught in a cycle where success became the ultimate measure of her worth, and failure—however small—felt like a personal defeat.

This self-imposed pressure was compounded by the external expectations placed upon her. As Emilie gained more visibility in the media and within her industry, the scrutiny of her personal life intensified. Public figures are often expected to maintain an image of flawlessness, and Emilie was no exception. The desire to live up to the ideal of a perfect, confident, and unshakable leader created a barrier between her true self and the image she projected to the world. In an effort to meet the expectations of her audience, Emilie began to suppress the personal struggles she was facing behind the scenes, afraid that showing vulnerability would diminish her credibility or professional standing.

While Emilie navigated the pressures of professional success, she also faced a series of personal losses that tested her resilience. The death of a close friend marked a significant turning point in her life. This loss, compounded by the emotional toll of balancing a high-powered career, caused Emilie to question everything. She struggled with grief, guilt, and the haunting thought that she wasn't able to fully process her emotions while being constantly in the spotlight. Emilie found herself questioning her capacity to continue at the same pace. How could she maintain the facade of having everything together when she was internally struggling to cope with such profound loss?

For a time, Emilie withdrew from her public life, stepping back from her usual commitments to focus on her personal healing. She realized that, in her quest for professional success, she had neglected to tend to her emotional health. This period of reflection allowed Emilie to confront the complexities of her own identity—who she was beyond the leader, the innovator, and the public figure. It became clear that in order to continue her professional journey with authenticity, she needed to first take the time to heal emotionally, rather than pushing through in silence.

The pressure to maintain a "perfect" image was not the only challenge Emilie faced behind the scenes; she also struggled with balancing her work and personal life. The demands of her career often left little time for the relationships she held dear—family, friends, and even herself. Emilie found herself increasingly isolated as she prioritized work over personal connections, convinced that success in her professional life would compensate for the sacrifices in her personal life. However, over time, she realized that the cost of neglecting these relationships was too high. Her sense of fulfillment was incomplete, as she had distanced herself from the very support system that had helped her reach her initial milestones.

Learning to restore these personal connections became a turning point for Emilie. She began to intentionally invest time in her relationships, setting boundaries to ensure that she could nourish both her career and her personal life. This balancing act was not easy, but Emilie learned that achieving success in one's career should not come at the expense of meaningful personal relationships. Through this shift in focus, Emilie found a renewed sense of purpose and fulfillment, understanding that true success encompasses both professional accomplishments and personal happiness.

Emilie also struggled with moments of self-doubt, despite her outward confidence. There were times when she questioned her ability to lead, whether she was doing enough to make a difference, and if she could continue to meet the demands of her career. These internal battles were at odds with the public persona she had cultivated—a persona that seemed to have it all together. Behind closed doors, Emilie had to confront her fears and uncertainties head-on, realizing that these feelings of self-doubt were natural and human, but they didn't define her capabilities. She learned to lean into her vulnerability, allowing herself to make mistakes, learn, and grow from them rather than seeing them as failures.

The personal challenges Emilie faced behind the scenes were integral to her growth as a leader and as a person. Through grief, self-doubt, and emotional struggle, she learned the importance of emotional resilience, self-compassion, and the ability to ask for help when needed. These experiences shaped her leadership style, making her more empathetic, authentic, and grounded. In the end, Emilie's ability to face and overcome these challenges behind the scenes allowed her to step into her full potential as both a leader and a human being, teaching her that true strength lies in the courage to be vulnerable, to embrace imperfection, and to prioritize what truly matters.

Coping with Public Expectations

As Emilie Kiser's career soared, so did the public's expectations of her. Gaining recognition and prominence in her field meant that Emilie was no longer just a private professional working behind the scenes—she had become a public figure, and with that came an overwhelming set of expectations that often felt impossible to meet. The scrutiny she faced was not just limited to her professional achievements but extended into her personal life, appearance, and every decision she made. Coping with these public expectations became one of the most challenging aspects of Emilie's journey, and it was a struggle that required her to constantly navigate the fine line between authenticity and the pressure to maintain an idealized image.

In the beginning, Emilie found the public's attention flattering. The recognition she received for her work was the result of years of dedication and hard work, and it was rewarding to see her efforts acknowledged. However, as her visibility grew, so did the expectations placed upon her. She was expected to be a role model, an impeccable leader, and a beacon of success at all times. The pressure to maintain this perfect image was immense, and Emilie quickly realized that the cost of such high expectations was beginning to take a toll on her mental and emotional well-being.

One of the most difficult aspects of coping with public expectations was the constant demand to present a flawless image. The media, colleagues, and even fans often saw her as an idealized figure—someone who always had the right answers, maintained an impeccable work-life balance, and exuded confidence and poise. Yet behind the scenes, Emilie was dealing with the same human struggles as anyone else. She grappled with feelings of self-doubt, exhaustion, and personal challenges, but she felt a profound pressure to conceal these vulnerabilities from the public eye. She feared that revealing her struggles would undermine her credibility and the image of success she had worked so hard to build.

This internal conflict was emotionally draining. Emilie felt torn between the persona she had cultivated for the public and her true, authentic self. The more she tried to meet the external expectations, the more disconnected she felt from her inner truth. She realized that trying to meet the public's image of perfection was not only unrealistic but also unsustainable. The emotional cost of constantly striving to meet these expectations began to overshadow the satisfaction she once found in her work and achievements.

The turning point came when Emilie finally acknowledged that the pursuit of perfection was not worth the toll it was taking on her mental health. She realized that she could not continue to live up to everyone else's standards and still remain true to herself. In an effort to cope with public expectations, Emilie began to embrace vulnerability and authenticity in her public persona. She made a conscious decision to show the more human side of herself—not just the polished, perfect leader but the person behind the accolades. She started to openly talk about her struggles, both personal and professional, and how she was learning to navigate the pressures of her career and the challenges of public life.

By being open about her own imperfections, Emilie was able to reclaim her sense of authenticity and reduce the burden of public scrutiny. She shared her experiences with burnout, self-doubt, and the difficulties of balancing her career with her personal life. Emilie became a more relatable figure, one who was not afraid to admit that she was still learning and growing, just like everyone else. Her vulnerability resonated with others, particularly young women who were facing similar pressures to perform and meet societal expectations. In doing so, Emilie shifted the narrative—she showed that success is not about being flawless, but about perseverance, resilience, and the courage to remain true to oneself despite the pressures of the world.

However, this shift in mindset did not come without its challenges. Emilie's decision to be more transparent about her struggles was met with mixed reactions. While many people appreciated her authenticity, others criticized her for being "too human" or "not living up to the ideal" they had come to expect. It was a painful realization that public perception would always be out of her control, and no matter how authentic she became, there would always be critics. But Emilie learned to embrace this fact. She understood that she couldn't please everyone, and trying to do so would only lead to burnout and dissatisfaction.

Over time, Emilie found that by setting boundaries and taking care of her mental health, she was better able to manage the weight of public expectations. She prioritized self-care, sought support when needed, and made a conscious effort to separate her self-worth from the opinions of others. She surrounded herself with a close circle of mentors, family, and friends who reminded her of her value beyond her public image. With this strong support system, Emilie was able to maintain a healthy perspective, recognizing that her success and worth were not defined by how others viewed her, but by the work she did and the impact she made.

Coping with public expectations was an ongoing challenge, but it became one of Emilie's greatest strengths. It taught her the importance of authenticity, vulnerability, and resilience. It helped her realize that true success comes not from meeting the world's expectations but from aligning her public persona with her core values and being true to who she was. Emilie's ability to navigate these pressures with grace and authenticity not only allowed her to maintain her success but also deepened her connection with others and reinforced her legacy as a leader who inspired with both her achievements and her humanity.

The Role of Family and Close Friends

Throughout her journey to success, Emilie Kiser has often credited her family and close friends as the foundation upon which her achievements were built. While her professional skills and personal resilience played significant roles in her rise, it was the unwavering support and guidance from the people closest to her that provided the strength she needed to navigate the inevitable challenges along the way. In a world where success is often viewed as a solo endeavor, Emilie's story is a testament to the power of connection, shared wisdom, and the importance of having a solid support system behind you.

From an early age, Emilie's family was the bedrock of her development. Her parents, each with their own unique strengths, instilled in her the values of hard work, integrity, and perseverance. Her mother, a figure of strength and determination, taught her the importance of self-sufficiency and independence. She was a woman who balanced a demanding career with raising children, and her example left an indelible mark on Emilie. Emilie admired how her mother made no compromises when it came to her professional goals while maintaining a warm and nurturing home environment. It was from her mother that Emilie learned the invaluable lesson of never settling for less, of pursuing her dreams while still maintaining the balance and stability of a well-rounded life.

Her father, equally influential, provided Emilie with a steady and grounded perspective. With his wisdom and calm demeanor, he taught her the importance of long-term vision and the patience required to achieve lasting success. Her father encouraged her to think critically, to ask questions, and to remain steadfast in the face of adversity. His guidance was a constant source of support throughout Emilie's career, particularly when she faced moments of self-doubt or questioned whether she was on the right path. Emilie's parents were not only role models but also her first mentors—people whose love and commitment helped her build the confidence to step into the leadership roles she would later occupy.

As Emilie grew older and began to carve out her own career, her relationship with her family evolved into one of mutual respect and admiration. She continued to lean on them for advice, emotional support, and perspective. The importance of her family in keeping her grounded cannot be overstated. In an industry where the pursuit of success often leads to personal sacrifice, Emilie's family was her anchor, reminding her of her roots and the values that would always define her.

Equally important to Emilie's success were her close friends— those who provided not just professional guidance but also emotional support when she needed it most. These friendships, forged through shared experiences and mutual respect, became her safe haven in times of stress and uncertainty. In a world that often prioritizes competition, Emilie's closest friends were a source of encouragement, understanding, and unconditional support. These friends were not just passive observers of her success; they were active participants in her life, offering advice, challenging her ideas, and helping her stay true to her values.

Friendship, for Emilie, became a crucial tool for personal growth. While her family offered unwavering support, it was her friends who often helped her process the complexities of her professional life. They were the ones who would listen patiently when Emilie vented about the pressures of public scrutiny, the difficulty of maintaining a work-life balance, or the isolation that sometimes accompanies success. It was through these friendships that Emilie found the space to express her vulnerabilities and, in doing so, gained the strength to overcome her personal and professional struggles. Her friends held a mirror to her, showing her not just her achievements but also her potential and the value she brought to those around her.

The role of family and close friends in Emilie's life is a reminder that success is not achieved in isolation. While hard work, perseverance, and personal resilience are critical components of any career, it is the emotional and psychological support from those we trust that allows us to thrive in a world that can often feel overwhelming. Emilie's story is a testament to the importance of building meaningful, supportive relationships and cultivating a network of people who will not only celebrate your victories but help you navigate the inevitable setbacks along the way.

For Emilie, her family and close friends have been both a sounding board and a source of unwavering strength. They have celebrated her achievements, supported her during her lowest moments, and reminded her of her worth when the world seemed to question it. In every success she achieved, Emilie has always acknowledged that the love, encouragement, and wisdom from her family and friends were instrumental in getting her to where she is today. Their support has allowed her to stay grounded, remain true to herself, and ultimately build a legacy not just based on professional success, but on the enduring bonds of love and friendship that have sustained her throughout her journey.

Resilience and Overcoming Adversity

Resilience is often defined as the ability to bounce back from adversity, to recover and thrive despite the challenges that life throws at you. For Emilie Kiser, resilience has been a cornerstone of her success, a thread woven through every aspect of her career and personal life. Her journey has not been without its hardships, and she has faced many obstacles that could have derailed her progress. However, it was her ability to confront these challenges head-on, learn from them, and keep moving forward that has shaped her into the strong, accomplished leader she is today. This chapter delves into Emilie's experiences with adversity and how her resilience enabled her to not only survive but ultimately thrive.

One of the first major adversities Emilie encountered was during her early years in the professional world. As a young woman entering a competitive and male-dominated industry, Emilie quickly learned that success would not come easily. She faced both overt and subtle forms of discrimination, with colleagues questioning her abilities simply because of her gender. At times, her ideas were dismissed, or her contributions were undermined, forcing her to constantly prove herself. In the face of these challenges, Emilie could have easily become discouraged, but instead, she used them as fuel to push harder. Rather than retreating in the face of adversity, she took it as an opportunity to demonstrate her worth through action.

Emilie's resilience during these formative years was shaped by her unwavering belief in herself and her abilities. She understood that while the external world might impose limitations on her, her internal strength and determination were the driving forces that would propel her forward. She began to focus on honing her skills, becoming an expert in her field, and consistently delivering results that couldn't be ignored. In doing so, she earned the respect of those around her—not by seeking validation but by proving her capabilities through her work.

Another significant challenge that tested Emilie's resilience came later in her career, when she was tasked with leading a major project that was struggling to find direction. The project was behind schedule, morale was low, and there were high stakes for the company. Emilie could have easily stepped aside or allowed the situation to overwhelm her, but instead, she embraced the challenge with determination. She took a step back to assess the situation, redefined the strategy, and inspired her team to work together toward a common goal. Despite the many setbacks and obstacles along the way, Emilie's resilience allowed her to turn the project around, achieving success where many thought failure was inevitable. This moment of overcoming adversity not only showcased her leadership abilities but also reinforced her belief in her capacity to rise above difficult circumstances.

In addition to professional challenges, Emilie has also faced personal hardships that tested her emotional strength. One of the most profound struggles in her life was the loss of a close family member. The grief she felt was overwhelming, and it came at a time when her career was demanding more of her attention than ever. The weight of balancing personal loss with professional responsibilities was almost too much to bear. However, Emilie did not allow this setback to define her. Instead, she leaned into the support of her family and close friends and took the time she needed to grieve and heal. Her ability to process this loss, without letting it derail her, was a testament to her emotional resilience. She learned that resilience isn't just about pushing through—it's about knowing when to step back, regroup, and come back stronger.

Moreover, Emilie's resilience has been crucial in her ability to adapt to the ever-changing demands of her career. As the professional world evolved, so did the challenges she faced. The rise of new technologies, shifting market trends, and changes in workplace culture all required Emilie to be flexible and open to learning. She faced moments of uncertainty, particularly as she transitioned into new roles and responsibilities, but her ability to embrace change and continue learning helped her stay ahead of the curve. She understood that the key to overcoming adversity was not to resist change but to adapt and grow from it. Emilie made it a point to stay curious, seek new knowledge, and apply innovative thinking to her work, which kept her at the forefront of her industry.

Through every adversity Emilie faced, she learned that resilience is not about being invincible or unaffected by challenges; it's about how you respond to those challenges. Resilience is the ability to persevere when the road gets tough, to learn from setbacks, and to use them as stepping stones rather than stumbling blocks. Emilie's resilience has been a driving force behind her success—allowing her to face obstacles with courage, bounce back from failure, and continue pushing toward her goals, no matter how difficult the journey. Her story is a powerful reminder that true success is not measured by the absence of challenges, but by the strength and determination to overcome them. Through her ability to face adversity with resilience,

Emilie has not only achieved professional success but also built a lasting legacy of perseverance, leadership, and personal growth.

Chapter 5
Impact on Her Field and Legacy

Emilie Kiser's journey has always been driven by the desire to create meaningful change—not just for herself, but for the industry and communities she serves. As her career progressed, it became clear that her contributions were not just about achieving personal success; they were about making an enduring impact on her field. From her innovative strategies to her leadership approach, Emilie's work has left an indelible mark on the industry, and her legacy continues to inspire and shape the next generation of professionals. This chapter delves into the ways in which Emilie's influence has shaped her field and the legacy she is building through her work, leadership, and advocacy.

Emilie's impact on her field began with her ability to think outside the box and challenge traditional norms. Early in her career, she demonstrated an exceptional ability to solve complex problems in creative ways, often seeing opportunities where others saw obstacles. Her work on major projects—especially those that had failed or were on the brink of failure—showcased her talent for innovation. She was not content to follow the established path; instead, she was always looking for new, more effective ways to approach challenges, and this mindset became one of her defining characteristics. Through her leadership and problem-solving abilities, Emilie redefined what was possible within her industry, setting new standards for success and paving the way for others to follow in her footsteps.

One of the key areas where Emilie's impact is particularly profound is in leadership and team development. Throughout her career, Emilie was not just a manager—she was a mentor, guiding and empowering those around her to reach their fullest potential. She believed that great leaders are those who can elevate others, and she made it a priority to invest in the growth of her team members. Her focus on mentorship, collaboration, and empathy transformed the way leadership was perceived in her industry. Emilie's leadership style emphasized listening, inclusivity, and empowering others to take ownership of their work. This approach not only fostered strong, loyal teams but also resulted in improved performance and productivity across the board. Her leadership became a model for others to emulate, and her influence in this area continues to be felt through the professionals she mentored and the organizations she helped shape.

Beyond her direct work and leadership, Emilie's advocacy for diversity and inclusion has left a lasting legacy in her field. Early on, she recognized the importance of creating spaces where all voices could be heard, particularly those that had historically been marginalized. Whether advocating for women in leadership, supporting underrepresented communities, or pushing for equitable workplace practices, Emilie made it her mission to use her position to affect systemic change. She became a vocal champion for gender equality and diversity, not just within her own company, but across the industry. Emilie's advocacy has inspired many to take similar stands for inclusivity, and her work continues to challenge outdated norms and encourage organizations to prioritize diversity in all its forms.

Emilie's impact on her field also extends to the broader community. She has consistently used her platform to address important societal issues and advocate for causes she deeply cares about. From her involvement in community outreach initiatives to her work on promoting education and equal opportunities, Emilie has demonstrated that professional success is not just about personal gain but also about making a difference in the world. Through her charitable work, she has become an example of how leadership can be used as a tool for social good. Emilie's contributions go beyond the boardroom—they reach into the lives of individuals and communities who benefit from her advocacy and support.

The legacy that Emilie is building is multifaceted—one defined by her groundbreaking professional achievements, her transformative leadership, and her commitment to creating positive change in society. Her work has set new benchmarks for excellence in her field, and her influence extends far beyond her immediate industry. As more professionals look to Emilie's career as a model for success, her legacy continues to inspire those who want to make a lasting impact on their communities and industries. Her story shows that true success is not simply about achieving personal milestones; it is about leaving behind a trail of positive change, empowering others to rise to their full potential, and creating a future where success is not measured solely by individual accomplishments but by the collective progress of society.

As this chapter unfolds, we will explore the specific ways in which Emilie's contributions have shaped her field, how she has mentored and inspired others, and the lasting legacy she is leaving behind. Emilie's impact is not confined to the work she has done but extends to the people she has touched and the lasting changes she has inspired. Through her innovative thinking, her leadership, and her unwavering commitment to social justice, Emilie Kiser's legacy is one that will continue to influence and inspire for years to come.

Contributions to Her Industry

Emilie Kiser's contributions to her industry have been nothing short of transformative. From the moment she entered the professional world, she demonstrated an exceptional ability to innovate, lead, and challenge the status quo. Her work has redefined what success looks like within her field, pushing boundaries and introducing new ideas that have not only shaped the industry's current landscape but have also laid the foundation for its future growth and evolution. Emilie's influence can be seen in her groundbreaking work, her leadership style, and her advocacy for inclusivity and diversity, which have collectively changed the way the industry operates and how professionals in the field approach their work.

One of Emilie's most significant contributions has been her ability to drive innovation within her industry. Early in her career, she identified areas where traditional methods and strategies were falling short. Rather than following the conventional path, Emilie took a bold approach by introducing new ideas that challenged the established norms. One of her key innovations was her ability to blend creative strategies with data-driven decision-making. While many in her industry relied on traditional marketing and sales strategies, Emilie integrated cutting-edge technologies and analytical tools to optimize performance, improve customer engagement, and drive sales. Her approach to leveraging data in creative ways set a new benchmark for how businesses could use technology to enhance their strategies, resulting in more targeted and efficient marketing campaigns.

Emilie's focus on innovation didn't stop at the technical level; she also revolutionized the way teams approached problem-solving and collaboration. Her leadership style emphasized the importance of collective intelligence and the power of collaboration. In an industry that had often been competitive and siloed, Emilie fostered a culture of inclusivity and cooperation within her teams. She recognized that true innovation comes from diverse perspectives, and she made it a priority to build teams that brought different skills, backgrounds, and ideas to the table. This not only led to more creative solutions but also encouraged a sense of ownership and commitment among her team members. Emilie's leadership style became a model for others in the industry, with many following her example of empowering teams to take risks and experiment with new ideas.

Another major contribution Emilie made to her industry was her work in transforming how businesses approached diversity and inclusion. Throughout her career, she has been an outspoken advocate for creating more inclusive workplaces where people from all backgrounds feel valued and supported. In an industry that has historically struggled with diversity, Emilie was determined to be a catalyst for change. She worked tirelessly to implement policies and practices that promoted equity and opportunity, both within her own organization and across the industry at large. Emilie's efforts to advocate for greater diversity have been instrumental in opening doors for underrepresented groups, particularly women and minorities, to access leadership roles and have a seat at the table in decision-making processes. Her advocacy work has also helped to shift the industry's mindset, encouraging companies to recognize the value of diverse perspectives and how they contribute to innovation, creativity, and better business outcomes.

Emilie's commitment to creating inclusive spaces within her industry was not just about speaking out—it was about creating tangible, lasting change. She initiated mentorship programs aimed at helping women and minority professionals develop the skills and confidence needed to advance in their careers. She also partnered with various organizations to create educational programs and workshops that focused on leadership development, diversity, and inclusion. Through these efforts, Emilie empowered others to take on leadership roles and break through the barriers that had previously held them back. Her work in this area has left a lasting impact on the industry, fostering an environment where talent is recognized regardless of background, and diversity is seen as an asset rather than a challenge.

In addition to her work on diversity and innovation, Emilie has contributed to the broader industry by mentoring emerging leaders. She has been a consistent source of guidance for young professionals, offering advice and support on navigating the complexities of career growth. By sharing her experiences, both the successes and the challenges, Emilie has helped to shape the next generation of leaders who will continue to push the industry forward. Her commitment to mentorship and developing talent is one of the reasons why her impact on the industry will continue long after her time in the spotlight has passed.

Emilie's contributions to her industry extend beyond her direct work and leadership; they are embedded in the culture she has helped to create. Through her focus on innovation, collaboration, and inclusivity, Emilie has transformed not only the organizations she's been a part of but the entire industry. She has shown that true leadership is about creating a lasting, positive impact that transcends personal achievements and extends to the broader community.

Emilie's legacy in the industry is one of progress, empowerment, and a commitment to creating spaces where all individuals have the opportunity to thrive. Through her groundbreaking work and her unwavering dedication to making a difference, Emilie Kiser has not only changed the trajectory of her own career but has also shaped the future of the industry as a whole.

How Emilie Kiser Changed the Game

Emilie Kiser's impact on her industry goes beyond just her accomplishments—it lies in how she fundamentally altered the way business is conducted, how leadership is perceived, and how innovation is integrated into every facet of professional work. She didn't just follow trends or adapt to the existing rules; Emilie rewrote them, creating new standards that have left a lasting imprint on the industry. Her ability to challenge norms, break barriers, and inspire change is why she is considered a game-changer in her field.

One of the most profound ways Emilie changed the game was through her innovative approach to leadership. Early in her career, she recognized that traditional leadership styles, which were often hierarchical and rigid, didn't align with her vision for how teams should operate. She understood that in order to foster true innovation and creative problem-solving, leadership had to be collaborative, inclusive, and empowering. Instead of imposing directives from the top down, Emilie embraced a more democratic and team-oriented leadership style, where every voice was valued. She fostered environments where team members were encouraged to take initiative, share their ideas, and work together toward common goals. This shift away from command-and-control management to a more fluid and inclusive style not only boosted morale but also led to better decision-making and more successful outcomes.

Emilie's leadership also placed a strong emphasis on mentorship. She didn't just seek to lead teams; she sought to develop future leaders. Early in her career, she noticed that women and minorities were underrepresented in leadership positions, and she made it her mission to change that. She launched initiatives aimed at creating pathways for underrepresented groups to rise into leadership roles, offering mentorship, training programs, and career development resources. Her commitment to diversity and inclusion created a ripple effect within the industry, encouraging other leaders to recognize the importance of fostering diverse talent and promoting equity within the workplace.

Beyond leadership, Emilie changed the way innovation was approached in her industry. In an environment that often relied on traditional methods and outdated systems, Emilie introduced new ways of thinking about problem-solving. She was not afraid to challenge the status quo or to experiment with new tools and technologies. Her ability to blend creative thinking with data-driven strategies allowed her to see opportunities where others saw obstacles. Emilie didn't just improve existing systems; she reinvented them. Her work with digital tools, data analytics, and customer-centric strategies transformed the way companies approached marketing, customer relations, and product development. By integrating these modern solutions into her strategies, Emilie created more efficient, impactful, and scalable results.

Another key aspect of Emilie's game-changing approach was her commitment to work-life balance, which became a part of her leadership ethos. In a field where long hours and burnout were often glorified, Emilie championed the importance of mental health, personal well-being, and self-care. She understood that true success couldn't be measured just by output or achievements; it had to take into account the holistic well-being of individuals. By prioritizing her own health and encouraging her team to do the same, Emilie set a new standard for what a healthy, sustainable work culture should look like. Her emphasis on balance didn't just lead to better performance; it contributed to happier, more engaged teams that felt supported and valued.

Moreover, Emilie's strategic approach to innovation didn't just transform her workplace—it also had a lasting impact on the industry as a whole. Her ability to envision the future of her field, anticipate changes, and position herself and her company for success ahead of the curve gave her a competitive edge that many others lacked. She was never content with following trends; she was always focused on creating them. By combining her forward-thinking strategies with an unwavering commitment to inclusivity and collaboration, Emilie became a driving force behind the industry's evolution.

Perhaps one of the most important ways Emilie changed the game was through her dedication to making a broader societal impact. While many leaders focus solely on their company's bottom line, Emilie consistently used her platform to address pressing social issues. From advocating for gender equality in the workplace to promoting diversity and inclusion across the industry, Emilie used her voice and influence to spark change beyond her immediate professional realm. She believed that success should not only be measured in profits but in the positive impact one can make on society. Her advocacy work continues to inspire future leaders to not only excel professionally but to also make meaningful contributions to the greater good.

Emilie Kiser's ability to challenge the norms, innovate, and inspire change has permanently altered the way business is done in her field. She redefined leadership, set new standards for innovation, and introduced a culture of inclusivity and well-being that has become integral to the modern workplace. Through her contributions, Emilie didn't just change the game—she reshaped it, leaving a legacy of progress, empowerment, and transformation that will continue to influence generations of leaders to come.

Recognition from Peers and Mentors

Emilie Kiser's rise to prominence was not only driven by her own skills and determination but also by the recognition she garnered from the peers and mentors who saw her potential and helped guide her along the way. These relationships played an integral role in her journey, providing both validation and invaluable advice that propelled her to higher levels of success. Recognition from those she admired and respected became not just a source of personal pride but also a testament to the impact she was having within her industry.

Early in her career, Emilie found herself surrounded by mentors who recognized her abilities and were eager to help her develop into a future leader. These mentors, individuals who had walked the path she was now on, offered Emilie insights into the complexities of the industry and helped her refine her professional skills. They provided wisdom, not only on the technical aspects of her work but also on the broader challenges of leadership, career development, and navigating the professional landscape. These early relationships became the foundation of Emilie's success, as the advice and guidance she received allowed her to avoid common pitfalls and stay focused on her long-term goals.

One of the most significant contributions of her mentors was helping Emilie understand the importance of networking and building strong professional relationships. As she entered new roles and faced more complex projects, Emilie's mentors encouraged her to expand her circle of influence, to seek out the advice and support of others who had experienced similar challenges. Through their guidance, Emilie learned how to leverage her professional network to gain new opportunities, receive constructive feedback, and collaborate with others who could contribute to her growth. This network of mentors, advisors, and peers became a vital resource that not only helped Emilie grow professionally but also made her feel more confident in her ability to succeed.

As Emilie continued to excel in her field, her peers began to take notice of her accomplishments. In a competitive industry where every move is scrutinized, the recognition from her colleagues was a testament to her abilities as a leader and innovator. Many of the individuals she worked with admired her work ethic, her ability to solve complex problems, and her unwavering dedication to excellence. As a result, Emilie found herself being invited to speak at industry events, collaborate on high-profile projects, and participate in discussions that would shape the future of her industry. Her peers recognized that she was not only capable of leading projects but also of driving change and challenging the status quo. Their recognition allowed Emilie to expand her influence, taking on leadership roles that would have seemed out of reach earlier in her career.

However, it was not just her professional recognition that mattered—it was also the personal validation she received from her peers. In a field where competition can sometimes create barriers between individuals, Emilie's ability to foster collaboration and build strong, trusting relationships with her colleagues set her apart. She was seen not only as a competent professional but as a person who genuinely cared about the success and well-being of those around her. This camaraderie and mutual respect created an environment where

Emilie could thrive, knowing that she had the support of her peers and that her contributions were truly valued.

Equally important was the recognition Emilie received from industry leaders and influential figures who became her mentors throughout her career. These high-level mentors saw something special in Emilie early on and chose to invest in her growth. They offered her opportunities that challenged her and helped her hone her skills, sometimes even putting her in positions where she had to step outside her comfort zone. These mentors, many of whom were established professionals with decades of experience, played a crucial role in helping Emilie navigate the complexities of leadership, influence, and decision-making.

For Emilie, the recognition from her mentors and peers was both humbling and motivating. It was a reflection of the respect she had earned through hard work, innovation, and a commitment to excellence. But it was also a reminder that success is not achieved alone. The recognition she received was a testament to the collaborative nature of her career, where mentorship, support, and teamwork had all played pivotal roles in her growth. Emilie understood that while her personal achievements were important, the people who had believed in her and guided her along the way had a significant hand in her success.

Over time, Emilie's peers and mentors began to view her not only as a rising star but as someone who could offer valuable insights and guidance to others. As she became more established in her field, she found herself in the position of mentor to younger professionals, offering the same support and wisdom that she had received early in her career. This full-circle moment was deeply meaningful for Emilie, as it allowed her to give back to the industry and help shape the next generation of leaders.

In the end, recognition from peers and mentors was not just a marker of Emilie's success; it was an acknowledgment of the integrity, leadership, and collaboration that had defined her career. It was the recognition of her ability to influence, inspire, and create change—both within her organization and in the broader industry. Through the relationships she built, the guidance she received, and the respect she earned, Emilie Kiser solidified her place as a leader whose impact would continue to be felt for years to come.

Lasting Effects on the Industry and Community

Emilie Kiser's influence on her industry and the broader community extends far beyond her personal achievements and success. Her legacy is shaped not just by the work she did within her professional sphere, but by the lasting changes she made in the way business is conducted, how leaders approach their roles, and how communities and organizations can work toward a more inclusive and equitable future. Emilie's efforts have had a profound and far-reaching effect, and her impact continues to resonate, setting new standards for excellence, leadership, and social responsibility in her industry and beyond.

One of the most significant ways Emilie has left a lasting impact on the industry is through her approach to leadership. She revolutionized the concept of leadership by emphasizing collaboration, transparency, and inclusivity. In an industry that had traditionally relied on hierarchical, top-down management structures, Emilie introduced a more democratic and people-centered model. She believed that leadership wasn't about authority or control but about empowering others to succeed. By promoting mentorship, cross-functional collaboration, and diversity of thought, she helped create environments where teams were encouraged to innovate and take risks. This shift in leadership dynamics not only improved organizational performance but also set a new benchmark for how leadership should be practiced across industries. Emilie's leadership philosophy has since become a cornerstone for companies looking to build resilient, forward-thinking teams capable of navigating the complexities of a rapidly changing world.

Beyond leadership, Emilie's commitment to diversity and inclusion has had an enduring impact on the industry. Throughout her career, she was a passionate advocate for equal opportunities, particularly for women and minorities, in leadership roles. She recognized early on that the lack of diversity in her field was not only limiting the potential of individuals but also stifling innovation and progress. Emilie took proactive steps to create inclusive spaces, develop mentorship programs, and push for policies that would level the playing field for underrepresented groups. Her efforts have contributed to a broader cultural shift within the industry, encouraging companies to prioritize diversity, not just as a moral imperative but as a business strategy that drives creativity, innovation, and sustainable growth.

Emilie's impact on the community is equally significant. Her work went beyond professional success; it was always about creating a meaningful and positive difference in the lives of others. Emilie used her platform and influence to support causes she was passionate about, particularly those related to education, empowerment, and social justice. She worked with nonprofit organizations, mentored young professionals, and advocated for policies that would create opportunities for individuals from all backgrounds to succeed. By focusing on community engagement, Emilie demonstrated that success is not just about individual achievement but about lifting others up along the way. Through her charitable efforts, Emilie not only changed the lives of individuals within her own network but also contributed to creating more equitable communities, where opportunity is available to everyone, regardless of their background or circumstances.

Her influence also extends to the next generation of leaders. As a mentor and role model, Emilie has inspired countless young professionals, particularly women and people of color, to pursue careers in leadership and innovation. By sharing her experiences, both the successes and the challenges, she has shown others that it is possible to break through barriers, challenge expectations, and achieve greatness. Emilie's mentorship programs, speaking engagements, and personal guidance have equipped the next wave of leaders with the tools and knowledge they need to succeed. Many of her mentees have gone on to become influential figures in their own right, continuing Emilie's legacy of fostering diverse, innovative, and empowered leadership.

Emilie's contributions to both the industry and the community have been instrumental in creating a more inclusive, dynamic, and resilient environment for future generations. Her legacy is not defined by her personal success but by the lasting changes she initiated—changes that have transformed the way business is done, how leaders view their roles, and how communities approach issues of equality and opportunity. Her work has helped pave the way for a new era of leadership that values diversity, collaboration, and social responsibility, creating a ripple effect that will continue to inspire and influence leaders for years to come.

As Emilie's career continues to evolve, her impact will be felt across multiple sectors, from business and leadership to education and social justice. The lasting effects of her work, both within her industry and her community, are a testament to the power of one individual's ability to spark change, challenge the norms, and leave behind a legacy that transcends professional accomplishments. Through her commitment to innovation, inclusivity, and empowerment, Emilie Kiser has created a future where leaders not only strive for success but also for positive, lasting change that benefits everyone.

Chapter 6
Public Perception and Media Influence

As Emilie Kiser's career flourished and her influence grew, the media became an inescapable part of her journey. Her accomplishments, leadership, and advocacy efforts garnered increasing attention, and soon, she found herself in the spotlight. Public perception, shaped largely by media portrayal, became an important aspect of Emilie's career, impacting both her professional opportunities and personal experiences. This chapter explores the ways in which media influence shaped Emilie's public image, the challenges she faced in managing her narrative, and the role public perception played in defining her legacy.

In the early stages of her career, Emilie was able to focus on her work without the overwhelming presence of the media. However, as she achieved more success, she quickly realized that her accomplishments would attract the public's attention. Media outlets began to cover her projects, celebrate her innovations, and highlight her leadership achievements. While this recognition was flattering, it soon became clear that being in the public eye came with a double-edged sword. On the one hand, the media provided Emilie with a platform to amplify her message, advocate for causes she believed in, and inspire others. On the other hand, it exposed her to scrutiny, judgment, and an often unrealistic portrayal of her life.

For Emilie, managing public perception required a delicate balance. The media's portrayal of successful individuals can sometimes be both empowering and limiting. As a prominent leader in her field, Emilie found herself subject to the expectations of perfection that often come with fame. The pressure to present an image of unshakable confidence and flawless success became overwhelming at times. Media coverage frequently focused on her professional achievements, but the personal toll of juggling her career, relationships, and well-being was rarely acknowledged. Emilie quickly learned that her public image, shaped by the media, was often disconnected from the complexity of her real-life experiences.

Navigating this tension between public perception and reality became one of Emilie's most significant challenges. As she gained more visibility, the media spotlight intensified, and so did the expectations placed upon her. The pressure to maintain an idealized version of herself led Emilie to reconsider how she wanted to be seen by the public. Rather than conforming to the conventional standards of success that the media often glorified, she chose to take control of her narrative and present a more authentic version of her journey. Emilie made the conscious decision to be transparent about the challenges she faced, both personally and professionally. By sharing her struggles with her audience—whether it was the toll of burnout, moments of self-doubt, or the emotional impact of personal losses—Emilie humanized herself in a way that resonated deeply with others.

This shift in approach allowed Emilie to redefine her relationship with the media. Rather than being defined by the stories the press told about her, she chose to tell her own story. Through interviews, public speaking engagements, and social media, Emilie began to use her platform not just to promote her achievements but also to advocate for the things that mattered most to her. She spoke out on issues such as gender equality, diversity, mental health, and work-life balance, using her visibility to bring attention to causes that were often overlooked in the mainstream media. By being vulnerable and authentic, Emilie was able to create a more meaningful connection with her audience, one that went beyond her professional success and resonated on a personal level.

However, this strategy of authenticity did not come without its challenges. The media's focus on personal struggles or moments of vulnerability often led to criticism, with some questioning whether Emilie's openness about her difficulties undermined her credibility as a leader. Critics argued that being too transparent could harm her professional image, especially in an industry that often values strength and perfection over vulnerability. Yet, Emilie's decision to remain true to herself despite this scrutiny ultimately strengthened her public persona. She became known not just for her achievements but for her courage to speak openly about the complexities of leadership and success, something that set her apart from others in her field.

Emilie's experience with public perception and media influence has been a defining aspect of her career, and one that has shaped how she approaches her work and public life. She learned that while the media could amplify her voice and bring attention to important issues, it could also create unrealistic expectations and magnify her flaws. Navigating this complex relationship required resilience, self-awareness, and a deep commitment to her values. Emilie's ability to manage her image, stay grounded, and use the media to further her message of authenticity, inclusivity, and empowerment allowed her to not only thrive professionally but also leave a lasting impact on her industry and the communities she served.

In this chapter, we will explore the evolution of Emilie's relationship with the media, how public perception influenced her career trajectory, and the ways in which she used media attention to advocate for change. We will examine the challenges and rewards of living under the scrutiny of the public eye and how Emilie's approach to managing her image allowed her to maintain authenticity while navigating the pressures of fame. Through her experience, Emilie has demonstrated that while the media can shape public perception, true power lies in one's ability to control their own narrative and remain true to their values in the face of external pressures.

Media's Portrayal of Emilie Kiser

As Emilie Kiser's career advanced and her influence expanded, her presence in the media grew alongside it. The media, which had once celebrated her as a rising star in her field, now played a significant role in shaping her public image. While the attention was flattering, Emilie quickly realized that the media's portrayal of her, like that of many public figures, often came with a certain level of complexity. The narratives built around her achievements, personal life, and leadership style were not always a reflection of her true self but rather the idealized version that the media chose to highlight. This chapter explores how the media portrayed Emilie Kiser, the impact of this portrayal, and the challenges it presented as she navigated the public eye.

The media's initial portrayal of Emilie was largely focused on her professional achievements. As she began to gain recognition for her innovative strategies and leadership in her field, the press embraced her as a symbol of success—a determined, intelligent, and accomplished woman who had defied expectations to rise to the top of a competitive industry. Articles and interviews often highlighted her business acumen, her creative approach to problem-solving, and her ability to turn struggling projects into success stories. This portrayal was in many ways accurate, as Emilie had worked tirelessly to build a career founded on resilience, intelligence, and a commitment to excellence. However, this portrayal often painted her success as a smooth, linear progression, glossing over the personal and professional struggles that were an essential part of her journey.

As Emilie's visibility grew, so did the media's focus on her personal life. While her professional accomplishments remained central to her story, the press began to probe deeper into aspects of her private world, from her relationships to her appearance and lifestyle. The pressure to maintain a flawless public image intensified, and Emilie found herself scrutinized for how she presented herself to the world. Media outlets often focused on her physical appearance, style choices, and social life, sometimes reducing her to an image of perfection, rather than a multi-dimensional individual with real human experiences. The constant focus on her looks and personal life was not only exhausting but also alienating for Emilie. She felt that the media's portrayal of her often detracted from the work and the message she was trying to convey.

The media's portrayal also frequently emphasized Emilie's role as a trailblazer for women in leadership, and while this aspect of her story was something she embraced, it also came with a double-edged sword. As a woman in a male-dominated industry, Emilie was often seen as a "role model" for other women aspiring to break barriers. While she was proud to inspire others, the constant spotlight on her gender sometimes overshadowed her accomplishments and framed her successes in a way that felt patronizing. Instead of simply being recognized for her innovative ideas and leadership skills, Emilie was often portrayed through the lens of gender—celebrated for her "exceptional" ability to succeed as a woman in a male-dominated field, which sometimes undermined her achievements. This type of portrayal, while well-meaning, felt limiting to Emilie, who preferred to be seen as a leader first and foremost, without the need for gender-based qualifiers.

As with many public figures, the media's portrayal of Emilie was not always positive. The pressure of being constantly in the public eye meant that even the slightest misstep or perceived flaw was magnified. Media outlets began to scrutinize her every move, from business decisions to personal interactions. The media often sensationalized her failures or moments of vulnerability, portraying her not as someone who learned from challenges but as someone whose mistakes could tarnish her image. This relentless scrutiny was exhausting for Emilie, especially since it focused on isolated incidents rather than her overall body of work. It created a sense of imbalance in how she was viewed—she was praised for her successes but also harshly criticized for her missteps, creating a public persona that was not entirely reflective of her true character.

The impact of this portrayal on Emilie was profound. Initially, she struggled with the disconnect between the public image the media created and her real-life experiences. She was acutely aware of the gap between the flawless leader the media celebrated and the complex, sometimes imperfect woman she saw in the mirror. This tension created a sense of internal conflict as she grappled with the desire to maintain her professional identity while also wanting to be authentic and true to herself. Over time, Emilie began to accept that the media's portrayal of her was not something she could entirely control, but that she had the power to redefine how she engaged with the public. She decided to use her platform to offer a more authentic version of herself, one that acknowledged both her successes and struggles, and she began to speak openly about the challenges she faced in both her professional and personal life.

In an effort to regain control of her narrative, Emilie shifted her approach to media interactions. She started to focus on the causes that mattered most to her—advocating for diversity, equality, and mental health awareness. Rather than allowing the media to define her by superficial standards, she used her visibility to promote her core values. Through interviews, articles, and public appearances, Emilie worked to ensure that her story was not just about the image the media had created, but about the impact she wanted to have on the world. By doing so, she was able to reclaim her narrative and use her media presence as a platform to inspire and effect positive change.

Ultimately, the media's portrayal of Emilie Kiser was both a reflection of her achievements and a challenge she had to navigate in order to maintain her authenticity. While the public's expectations and the media's focus on her image were difficult at times, Emilie's ability to adapt, stay grounded, and control her own narrative allowed her to move forward with purpose. Through it all, she remained committed to her values and goals, showing that the true measure of success lies not in how one is portrayed but in the lasting impact one leaves on the world.

Navigating Fame and Privacy

As Emilie Kiser's career soared, the delicate balance between fame and privacy became one of her most significant challenges. Rising to prominence in an era where media attention is omnipresent and personal lives are often subject to public scrutiny, Emilie found herself thrust into the spotlight. While her professional achievements and advocacy work were celebrated, the increased visibility brought with it a loss of privacy and an ever-growing public curiosity about her personal life. Navigating the demands of fame while maintaining a sense of personal privacy required resilience, self-awareness, and a commitment to protecting her well-being.

In the early stages of her rise, Emilie was excited about the recognition her work brought. The articles, interviews, and speaking engagements were a reflection of her hard work and determination. However, as her name became synonymous with success and leadership, she quickly realized that the spotlight came with a double-edged sword. The more visible she became, the more her personal life, choices, and even her appearance were scrutinized. What she once viewed as personal moments with family, friends, and even her own thoughts became potential fodder for public consumption. Emilie soon found herself confronted with the challenge of maintaining her professional identity while safeguarding her private life from the invasive nature of public curiosity.

The loss of privacy was especially felt in moments of vulnerability or personal struggle. Like many public figures, Emilie found that every mistake, misstep, or emotional difficulty was amplified in the media. When faced with personal challenges, whether they were related to family matters, relationships, or moments of self-doubt, Emilie realized that her emotional experiences were no longer her own. The pressure to maintain a polished, idealized version of herself at all times was immense, and at times, overwhelming. It felt as though her true self—beyond her professional persona—was constantly under public examination, leaving little room for mistakes or human imperfections.

Despite this, Emilie chose to be proactive about navigating the fine line between fame and privacy. She understood that, in the digital age, privacy could no longer be fully protected, but she decided to establish boundaries that allowed her to retain control over what the public knew about her. She began to carefully curate her interactions with the media and how much personal information she shared. Rather than allowing the media to dictate her narrative, Emilie took control by being selective about what she revealed. She spoke openly about certain aspects of her personal life, especially when it aligned with her advocacy work, but chose to keep other matters private.

One of Emilie's primary strategies for maintaining her privacy was focusing the public's attention on her professional achievements and the causes she cared about. She used her platform to advocate for social issues such as gender equality, diversity in leadership, and mental health, creating a narrative centered around her work and values. By doing so, she was able to direct the media's focus toward the issues that mattered most to her and away from the more invasive aspects of her personal life. This approach allowed Emilie to maintain a sense of agency over her public image, ensuring that her fame served as a vehicle for change and influence rather than simply being a spectacle for public consumption.

However, Emilie's efforts to protect her privacy didn't always shield her from the pressures of fame. There were times when she felt the weight of being constantly in the public eye, particularly when dealing with personal matters that were difficult to navigate. Yet, Emilie's approach to managing fame was rooted in authenticity. Rather than trying to maintain a perfect, untouchable image, she chose to be open about the challenges she faced, even when those challenges were deeply personal. She shared her struggles with mental health, work-life balance, and the emotional toll of public scrutiny, showing that vulnerability is not a weakness but a source of strength.

Emilie also learned the importance of creating a support system outside of the public sphere—family, close friends, and a small network of trusted colleagues. These relationships were crucial in helping her maintain a sense of normalcy and grounding amidst the pressures of fame. She realized that while her professional life was widely known, her personal life was hers to protect. By keeping her inner circle small and deeply connected, Emilie was able to shield herself from the noise of the public eye and focus on what truly mattered to her.

Over time, Emilie's ability to navigate fame and privacy became a key part of her resilience. She found ways to maintain her authenticity and purpose while protecting her personal life from undue scrutiny. She learned that fame, while offering incredible opportunities to influence and advocate for change, also required her to be discerning about what she shared and when. By setting clear boundaries and focusing on the work she was passionate about, Emilie was able to thrive in the public eye without losing herself in the process.

Emilie's story is a powerful example of how one can navigate the complexities of fame and privacy while staying true to one's values. Her ability to set boundaries, curate her public narrative, and maintain a sense of self in the face of external pressures has allowed her to continue to inspire others without sacrificing her personal peace. In a world where public figures are often expected to share every aspect of their lives, Emilie's approach offers a refreshing reminder that privacy and authenticity can coexist alongside fame.

The Role of Social Media in Shaping Her Image

In today's digital age, social media plays an undeniably powerful role in shaping public perceptions and building a personal brand. For Emilie Kiser, social media became both an opportunity and a challenge, a platform through which she could connect with her audience and amplify her message, but also a space where her image could be both curated and scrutinized. As her professional and public profile grew, social media emerged as a critical tool in defining how Emilie was perceived, offering a direct line to her audience but also exposing her to the sometimes harsh realities of public life.

From the outset, Emilie understood the power of social media as a tool for influence and engagement. As her career advanced, she realized that maintaining a controlled yet authentic presence on platforms like Instagram, Twitter, and LinkedIn was essential for connecting with her followers and staying relevant in an ever-evolving industry. Social media gave Emilie the opportunity to engage directly with her audience, share her insights, and present herself as both a leader and a thought leader. By sharing her professional milestones, speaking engagements, and innovative strategies, Emilie used social media to position herself as an authority in her field. It allowed her to be a part of important conversations, contribute to industry discourse, and advocate for causes she deeply cared about, such as diversity and inclusion, gender equality, and work-life balance.

However, social media also presented challenges when it came to controlling her narrative. As a public figure, Emilie was not immune to the scrutiny that comes with being on the world's most widely used platforms. Every post, tweet, or comment could be interpreted and shared by millions, with potential consequences for her personal and professional reputation. While social media gave Emilie a voice, it also magnified her actions—both positive and negative—on a global scale. The expectation for constant engagement and content creation became overwhelming at times, and Emilie often found herself walking a fine line between staying connected with her audience and protecting her personal boundaries.

In particular, social media presented a challenge in terms of balancing authenticity with the expectations of her audience. The pressure to maintain a polished, "perfect" image on social media, as is common with many influencers and public figures, was real. However, Emilie chose to buck this trend by focusing on authenticity. She recognized the importance of showing both her successes and her vulnerabilities. Rather than presenting an idealized version of herself, she used social media to share more than just her professional accomplishments. Emilie spoke openly about the struggles she faced, including the toll that public life and career pressures sometimes had on her mental health and well-being. She became a champion for showing the human side of leadership, acknowledging that it's okay to face setbacks and challenges along the way.

This transparency resonated with many of her followers, especially women and young professionals, who saw Emilie not as a perfect, unattainable figure but as someone they could relate to. She shared her journey with them—the difficulties, the wins, and everything in between—allowing her social media presence to become a source of both inspiration and genuine connection. Emilie's openness on these platforms not only helped to humanize her but also made her message about resilience, self-care, and breaking barriers more impactful.

The role of social media in shaping Emilie's image was also critical in amplifying her advocacy work. As a vocal advocate for diversity and inclusion, Emilie used her platforms to bring attention to the importance of equity in the workplace. She shared articles, wrote posts, and participated in discussions that centered on the need for systemic change in corporate structures and leadership. Through her social media presence, Emilie was able to reach a broader audience with her message, inspiring others to take action and support the causes she cared about. Her authenticity and commitment to these issues garnered respect from followers and peers alike, solidifying her reputation as not only a professional leader but a social leader.

Despite the positive impact, Emilie also experienced the challenges that come with the instant feedback and commentary that social media provides. Like many public figures, she faced criticism and judgment, some of which felt personal or unwarranted. The ability for anyone to comment on her posts, often with anonymity, meant that her every move could be scrutinized, misinterpreted, or criticized. While she initially struggled with this, Emilie eventually learned to compartmentalize and focus on the constructive feedback, while letting go of the negativity that did not serve her.

In navigating these challenges, Emilie also realized the importance of maintaining boundaries on social media. She became more deliberate about what she shared and how she engaged with her followers, recognizing that her mental health and personal life needed to be respected. She set clear boundaries about what she was willing to disclose, maintaining a sense of privacy and protecting her well-being while still staying engaged with her audience.

In summary, social media played a dual role in shaping Emilie Kiser's image. It offered a platform for sharing her professional successes and personal story while simultaneously exposing her to the challenges of public scrutiny. Through her transparency, authenticity, and commitment to advocacy, Emilie redefined how social media could be used not just for personal branding but also for inspiring change. By staying true to herself and using the platform responsibly, Emilie has turned social media into a tool for empowerment, connection, and leadership, all while maintaining a sense of balance and authenticity that resonates with her followers.

Public Support vs. Criticism

For Emilie Kiser, achieving success and prominence in her field has inevitably led to an overwhelming wave of both public support and criticism. The scrutiny of a public figure often comes with the territory of fame, and as Emilie's career flourished, she quickly found herself navigating the complex dynamics of being in the spotlight. While public recognition and admiration were deeply gratifying, they also came with the inevitable downside: criticism. For someone who had built her career on hard work, dedication, and a commitment to innovation, the challenge of managing both praise and negative feedback became an integral part of her journey. This chapter explores how Emilie has handled the balance between public support and criticism, and how these two forces have shaped her path.

Emilie's rise to prominence came with an overwhelming amount of public support. As she made waves in her industry, leading teams, driving innovation, and advocating for social causes, her work resonated deeply with others. The recognition she received—from colleagues, industry leaders, and the public—became a testament to the positive impact she had made. Emilie's story, especially as a woman breaking barriers in a male-dominated industry, inspired many. Her supporters lauded her for being a trailblazer, a mentor, and an advocate for diversity, and they were quick to praise her leadership style, creativity, and unwavering commitment to her values.

The messages of support she received were not just from fans, but also from fellow professionals who recognized the significance of her contributions. Her peers in the industry often celebrated her innovative ideas and the positive changes she had made in her workplace culture. Through social media, interviews, and speaking engagements, Emilie was able to connect with others who admired her work and looked up to her as a role model. This public support not only boosted her confidence but also reinforced her sense of purpose, knowing that her efforts were making a real difference in people's lives.

However, with the public support came criticism—something that every public figure must confront. As Emilie's visibility grew, so did the scrutiny of her every move. The more successful she became, the more vulnerable she became to judgment, both constructive and harsh. Criticism often focused on her leadership decisions, the methods she employed to achieve success, and even personal aspects of her life that the public had no right to judge. In an age where social media amplifies both positive and negative opinions, Emilie's every post, statement, or professional decision was met with a barrage of comments, some supportive and others downright hostile.

The criticism she faced was often grounded in her visibility as a woman in leadership. Some detractors questioned her ability to lead, attributing her success to external factors like her gender or her networking rather than acknowledging her competence, intelligence, and hard work. There were also moments when her actions were scrutinized to an extreme degree—her leadership decisions, personal choices, and even her appearance were picked apart. This constant public analysis, often based on limited or inaccurate information, left Emilie feeling vulnerable. Yet, rather than letting the negative feedback consume her, Emilie learned to develop a thicker skin and use criticism as an opportunity for growth.

Over time, Emilie began to embrace criticism as part of the process of public life, recognizing that it was an inevitable consequence of being visible. She understood that no matter how successful or impactful one's work may be, there will always be voices of dissent. Instead of allowing these voices to undermine her confidence, Emilie began to view criticism as a tool for reflection and improvement. She acknowledged that some feedback was valid and could be used to refine her leadership style or her approach to certain situations, while other feedback was simply rooted in jealousy, misunderstanding, or misinformation.

Emilie's ability to navigate public criticism became one of her greatest strengths. She learned not to take criticism personally but rather to assess it objectively, considering whether there was any merit to it that could help her evolve. In this way, she was able to turn negative feedback into a tool for self-improvement rather than letting it derail her progress. Additionally, Emilie began to focus on the positive, leaning into the support she received from her advocates and using it as a foundation to continue her work with passion and purpose.

What became clear over time is that public support, while incredibly uplifting, can also be fleeting. The admiration of others can be based on a momentary trend, a fleeting success, or a particular achievement. However, the ability to withstand and learn from criticism is what truly shapes lasting success. It is this combination of resilience and self-reflection that has allowed Emilie to not only overcome adversity but to continually rise above it. Her journey is a testament to the power of staying true to one's values, using both support and criticism to fuel growth, and always striving to make a meaningful impact despite the noise that often surrounds public life.

In the end, Emilie Kiser's approach to balancing public support and criticism has defined her path. She has shown that while the recognition of others is valuable, the true measure of success lies in one's ability to stay grounded, continue evolving, and maintain integrity in the face of both praise and adversity.

Chapter 7
The Personal Side of Emilie Kiser

Behind the professional achievements, public accolades, and industry leadership, there is a side to Emilie Kiser that is often overlooked: her personal life. While the media and public tend to focus on the successes and challenges of her career, the personal side of Emilie offers a deeper understanding of the woman behind the accolades. This chapter aims to explore the facets of Emilie's life that go beyond her professional persona, shedding light on her values, relationships, and the experiences that have shaped her as an individual.

Emilie Kiser's personal life is grounded in her core values of integrity, authenticity, and empathy. Throughout her career, she has remained fiercely true to these principles, both in her professional endeavors and in her personal relationships. Despite the pressures of fame, the demands of leadership, and the constant scrutiny of the public eye, Emilie has always prioritized staying connected to the things that matter most to her: her family, close friends, and personal well-being. For Emilie, success is not just about career accomplishments; it's about living a life that is balanced, meaningful, and aligned with her values.

A cornerstone of Emilie's personal life is her strong bond with her family. From an early age, she was taught the importance of hard work, resilience, and kindness by her parents, who instilled in her a deep sense of purpose. They were her first mentors, providing her with the foundation of wisdom and support that she would carry with her throughout her life. Emilie's relationship with her family continues to be a source of strength, offering her a sense of grounding amid the chaos of her professional life. They have been her unwavering supporters, offering advice, love, and a safe space in times of need. Her family's influence is evident in her approach to leadership, her emphasis on empathy in her professional relationships, and her commitment to making a positive impact on the lives of others.

In addition to her family, Emilie's close circle of friends plays a significant role in her personal life. These friendships provide her with a sense of normalcy and authenticity, offering moments of joy, laughter, and emotional connection outside of the demands of work. Emilie values her friendships deeply, knowing that the support and perspective they offer help her stay balanced and grounded. These relationships are a reminder that, despite the spotlight and professional recognition, she is first and foremost a person who cherishes human connection. Her friends have seen her at her most vulnerable, and it is through these personal connections that Emilie finds comfort and strength when faced with the challenges that come with public life.

Another important aspect of Emilie's personal life is her commitment to self-care and personal growth. While she is known for her hard work and dedication to her career, Emilie recognizes the importance of taking care of herself—both physically and mentally. She makes time for activities that nurture her well-being, whether it's exercise, reading, or simply spending time in nature. Emilie has been vocal about the need to prioritize mental health, particularly in high-pressure environments, and has openly discussed the importance of finding balance in her life. Her commitment to self-care is not only a reflection of her belief in the value of personal health but also an example she sets for others in her industry, showing that it's possible to achieve professional success without sacrificing personal happiness.

Despite the demands of her career, Emilie is also deeply involved in giving back to her community. She is passionate about supporting causes that align with her values, including education, diversity, and social justice. Emilie believes in using her platform for social good, advocating for those who may not have a voice and helping to create more equitable opportunities for others. Her personal commitment to social responsibility has been an integral part of her journey, allowing her to connect with individuals and organizations that share her passion for creating lasting change.

In exploring Emilie Kiser's personal life, it becomes clear that her success is not solely defined by the titles and accomplishments she has achieved in her career. Rather, it is her ability to balance the demands of a public career with her dedication to her family, friends, and personal well-being that truly defines who she is. Through her relationships, her commitment to self-care, and her passion for making a difference, Emilie has built a life that is rich with purpose and meaning. This personal side of Emilie offers a deeper, more nuanced understanding of the woman behind the professional accolades—one who values authenticity, human connection, and the pursuit of a balanced, fulfilled life.

Family Life and Relationships

Emilie Kiser's success in her professional life is often attributed to her determination, leadership, and drive, but the strong foundation of her family life and the deep relationships she has cultivated over the years have been just as integral to her achievements. Her family has been a constant source of support, offering her love, guidance, and perspective during both the highs and lows of her career. In a world where professional success often leads to personal sacrifices, Emilie has managed to maintain meaningful relationships and create a family dynamic that is centered around mutual respect, understanding, and unwavering support.

Emilie's relationship with her family has been one of her greatest sources of strength. Raised in a household that valued hard work, integrity, and compassion, she learned the importance of perseverance and the value of relationships early on. Her parents, in particular, played a pivotal role in shaping her worldview. They instilled in her the belief that success is not solely measured by career milestones but by the relationships you nurture and the values you uphold. Their wisdom and support laid the foundation for Emilie's approach to life—balancing personal fulfillment with professional ambition.

Her parents' influence continues to be evident in how Emilie navigates her own role as a professional and as a family member. Despite the demands of her career, Emilie always makes time for family, knowing that the love and support of those closest to her are vital for her emotional well-being. Whether it's spending quality time with her parents, siblings, or extended family, Emilie has built a life where her family is at the center. She maintains close, consistent communication with them, cherishing the connection that keeps her grounded in the face of public scrutiny and professional pressures.

In addition to her parents, Emilie's relationships with her siblings have also played a crucial role in her personal life. Growing up in a supportive, close-knit family, Emilie shares a deep bond with her siblings, who have been her confidantes, sounding boards, and sources of unconditional support. They have been there for her through every stage of her career, offering advice, celebrating her successes, and providing a sense of normalcy in her life. Emilie's siblings know her not just as a successful professional but as a person, and their ability to offer both emotional and practical support has helped her navigate the complexities of balancing family and career.

Emilie's romantic relationships, though not as publicized, have also been significant in shaping who she is today. As a highly successful woman in a demanding career, Emilie understands the importance of nurturing a balanced relationship where both partners are supportive of one another's goals and dreams. She has learned over time that being in a relationship doesn't mean compromising one's own aspirations, but rather finding a partner who respects and encourages personal growth while sharing in the joys and challenges of life. Her ability to maintain healthy, mutually supportive romantic relationships has been a key aspect of her personal well-being, allowing her to build a life that is rich with love and shared purpose.

Family life and relationships have also helped Emilie maintain perspective in moments of adversity. As her career progressed and public scrutiny intensified, it was her family and close friends who offered her a sense of stability and comfort. They provided a safe space where Emilie could express her vulnerabilities, decompress from the pressures of leadership, and regain the strength to continue pushing forward. Their unwavering belief in her, regardless of her public persona or professional setbacks, has been a source of resilience during difficult times.

Emilie's family life has also influenced her leadership style and how she interacts with her colleagues and teams. She recognizes the importance of creating supportive, inclusive work environments—ones that foster collaboration and care, much like the dynamic within her own family. Her approach to leadership, which emphasizes empathy, communication, and personal connection, is rooted in the values she learned from her family. She believes that nurturing strong relationships, both professionally and personally, is essential for long-term success. As a leader, Emilie strives to create a culture of respect and support, ensuring that those around her feel valued, heard, and motivated to contribute to shared goals.

Throughout her career, Emilie has been able to draw strength from her relationships and use her family's influence as a compass for navigating the complexities of public life. The unwavering support of her family and her commitment to maintaining meaningful relationships have not only been a source of comfort but have also fueled her ability to achieve greatness in her professional life. In balancing the demands of career and family, Emilie has shown that success is not just about professional accomplishments but about building a life that is rich with love, connection, and shared experiences.

Ultimately, Emilie Kiser's family life and relationships have been key to her overall success, providing the emotional support, grounding, and perspective necessary to thrive in both her personal and professional endeavors. Through her unwavering commitment to family, love, and connection, Emilie has built a legacy that transcends career milestones, leaving an impact on those around her and demonstrating that the most important success is found in the relationships we cultivate and the values we uphold.

Hobbies and Passions Beyond the Spotlight

While Emilie Kiser's professional life has been a testament to hard work, leadership, and innovation, the woman behind the accolades is more than just her career accomplishments. Beyond the spotlight, Emilie has a diverse range of hobbies and passions that provide her with both balance and fulfillment. These activities not only offer a much-needed reprieve from the pressures of her high-profile career but also reflect the deeper aspects of her personality — her creativity, compassion, and desire to live a well-rounded and meaningful life.

One of Emilie's greatest passions is her love for the arts, particularly visual arts and creative expression. Whether through painting, photography, or exploring various forms of visual storytelling, Emilie has always been drawn to artistic outlets that allow her to express herself in ways that are not tied to business or professional goals. Painting, in particular, has served as a therapeutic and meditative practice for Emilie. It's her way of disconnecting from the demands of her day-to-day life and reconnecting with her inner thoughts and emotions. The process of painting, where the act itself is as important as the end result, provides Emilie with a sense of peace and clarity. This creative outlet is a way for her to process complex emotions and find calm amidst the chaos of her busy schedule.

Alongside her artistic pursuits, Emilie has always had a passion for travel and exploration. She finds immense joy in experiencing new cultures, meeting people from diverse backgrounds, and gaining new perspectives. Whether for personal enrichment or as a way to expand her professional network, Emilie embraces the opportunity to immerse herself in different environments. Travel allows her to recharge, gain inspiration, and step outside the confines of her usual routine. Her adventures across the globe have not only broadened her worldview but have also provided her with a wealth of experiences that influence her work, particularly her advocacy for diversity and inclusivity. Through travel, Emilie gains insights into how different cultures approach leadership, work-life balance, and community-building, which she incorporates into her own philosophy and practices.

Another hobby that Emilie is deeply passionate about is fitness. As someone who has always been mindful of the importance of health, Emilie incorporates regular exercise into her routine, not only for physical benefits but also for mental clarity and emotional well-being. She enjoys activities such as hiking, yoga, and cycling, which allow her to stay active while also providing a sense of calm and mindfulness. Exercise, for Emilie, is not just about maintaining a healthy body, but also about nurturing her mental resilience and stress management. It provides her with the space to clear her mind, reflect on her goals, and recharge after demanding workdays. The balance of physical activity and mental focus plays an essential role in helping Emilie maintain a sense of equilibrium in her high-pressure environment.

Emilie is also an avid reader, and books have long been a source of both inspiration and escape for her. She has a particular fondness for biographies, historical novels, and books on personal development. Through reading, Emilie continues to expand her knowledge and understanding of the world, drawing inspiration from the lives of others, the lessons they have learned, and the challenges they have overcome. Books allow her to step into the lives of different individuals, giving her a sense of connection to humanity's shared experiences. For Emilie, reading is not just about learning; it's about gaining a deeper understanding of herself and the world around her, and finding ways to apply those insights in her own life.

Beyond her personal hobbies, Emilie is also deeply involved in giving back to the community. She is passionate about mentorship and has made it a priority to support young women and underrepresented individuals in the workforce. Whether through formal mentorship programs or informal advice, Emilie believes in the importance of lifting others as you rise. She enjoys hosting workshops, speaking at educational events, and supporting causes that promote social justice, education, and equal opportunities for all. Her dedication to helping others succeed, particularly those from marginalized communities, is not just a professional priority but a personal passion. By sharing her experiences and providing guidance, Emilie is able to make a meaningful impact on the next generation of leaders, helping them navigate the challenges she herself has overcome.

These hobbies and passions beyond the spotlight provide Emilie Kiser with a sense of fulfillment that goes beyond her professional identity. They allow her to stay grounded, tap into her creativity, and maintain a sense of balance amid the pressures of a demanding career. Through painting, traveling, fitness, reading, and giving back to her community, Emilie is able to cultivate a well-rounded life that not only supports her personal happiness but also enriches her professional endeavors. Her interests and passions remind her of the importance of staying connected to the things that bring joy and meaning, ensuring that her success is not just measured by career accomplishments, but by the depth and richness of her personal life.

What Emilie Kiser Values Most

Emilie Kiser's journey to success is not defined solely by her career achievements but also by the values she has upheld throughout her life. These principles have shaped how she approaches her work, her relationships, and the impact she has on the world. One of the core values that Emilie holds dear is integrity. She has always believed in doing what is right, even when it is difficult or inconvenient. Emilie's sense of integrity has guided her decisions, ensuring that her professional accomplishments are always in line with her moral compass. For Emilie, integrity is not just about adhering to ethical standards in business; it is about leading with honesty and authenticity, and inspiring others to do the same.

Another value that Emilie embodies is empathy. She has a deep understanding of the human experience and uses that empathy to connect with others in meaningful ways. Emilie's leadership style is centered around being compassionate and supportive, whether it's with her team, clients, or community. She recognizes the importance of listening and understanding others' perspectives, which has allowed her to create collaborative environments where individuals feel valued and heard. This empathy extends beyond the workplace as well. Emilie is deeply involved in social causes that align with her values, such as advocating for gender equality, diversity, and inclusion, and using her platform to fight for marginalized communities. Her passion for social justice is a direct result of her empathetic nature and desire to create a better, more equitable world.

Family plays a central role in Emilie's life. Despite the demands of her career, she has always made it a priority to maintain strong relationships with her family and close friends. Emilie credits her parents with instilling the values of hard work, perseverance, and kindness, which have been essential to her personal and professional success. Her family has been a constant source of support, offering her both love and guidance throughout her journey. Emilie understands the importance of nurturing these relationships, as they provide her with a sense of balance and stability, something that has allowed her to thrive in the often-chaotic world of business. Her commitment to her family ensures that her personal life remains grounded, even as her professional life continues to grow.

Continuous learning and personal growth are also central to Emilie's values. She firmly believes that the pursuit of knowledge is a lifelong process, one that never ends. Emilie embraces the idea that learning comes from both success and failure, and she strives to grow from each experience. Her commitment to self-improvement has driven her to seek out new opportunities for learning, whether through formal education, professional mentorship, or reading. This mindset has enabled her to stay at the forefront of her field, adapt to changing circumstances, and remain innovative in her work. Emilie also encourages others to adopt this mindset, believing that the key to long-term success is the ability to learn, evolve, and stay open to new ideas.

Giving back to the community is another value that Emilie holds close. Throughout her career, she has used her platform and influence to make a positive impact, especially in areas that align with her personal values. She believes that success should not only be measured by personal achievements but also by the difference one can make in the lives of others. Emilie has been involved in several initiatives to support underrepresented individuals in the workforce, particularly women and minorities. She actively mentors young professionals, offering advice, encouragement, and opportunities to help them succeed in their careers. Her dedication to creating a more inclusive and supportive environment for others is a testament to her belief in social responsibility and the importance of lifting others as you rise.

Lastly, Emilie values the importance of work-life balance and personal well-being. She understands that in order to excel in her career, she must first take care of herself. Whether through physical exercise, mental health practices, or spending time with loved ones, Emilie prioritizes her health and well-being. She knows that maintaining this balance allows her to bring her best self to both her personal life and her work. By taking time for self-care, Emilie ensures that she remains focused, resilient, and able to handle the demands of her professional life with clarity and purpose.

In conclusion, Emilie Kiser's values—integrity, empathy, family, continuous learning, social responsibility, and well-being—are the foundation of her success. These principles have guided her through the ups and downs of her career and life, helping her build a legacy that goes beyond professional achievements. Through her dedication to these values, Emilie has become a leader who not only excels in her field but also inspires others to lead with purpose, authenticity, and compassion.

Conclusion

Emilie Kiser's journey to success is a story of resilience, determination, and the unwavering commitment to her values. From her humble beginnings to becoming a trailblazer in her industry, her path has been shaped by hard work, personal struggles, and the support of the people around her. Along the way, Emilie has not only achieved remarkable professional accomplishments but has also made a profound impact on her industry and community. Her legacy is defined not just by her career milestones but by the values she has upheld, the relationships she has built, and the positive change she has inspired in others.

At the core of Emilie's story is the importance of authenticity. Throughout her career, she has consistently chosen to be true to herself, embracing both her strengths and vulnerabilities. This authenticity has allowed her to connect with others on a deeper level, whether through her leadership, her advocacy work, or her personal relationships. By being open about her struggles and triumphs, Emilie has shown that leadership is not about perfection but about embracing one's humanity and inspiring others through genuine, empathetic action. Her willingness to share her story has empowered countless individuals, particularly women and underrepresented groups, to break through barriers and pursue their own aspirations.

Emilie's ability to balance her professional success with her personal life is another defining aspect of her journey. Despite the demanding nature of her career, she has always prioritized her family, friendships, and personal well-being. This commitment to work-life balance has allowed her to maintain her sense of purpose and fulfillment, ensuring that her achievements are not solely defined by professional accolades but by the meaningful relationships and personal growth she has nurtured along the way. Emilie's story serves as a powerful reminder that success should not come at the cost of one's happiness, health, or the people who matter most.

In her professional life, Emilie has redefined leadership by emphasizing collaboration, inclusivity, and empowerment. Her innovative approach to leadership has not only transformed the organizations she has worked with but has also influenced the way businesses approach diversity, equity, and inclusion. Emilie has been a vocal advocate for creating environments where all individuals, regardless of their background, have the opportunity to succeed. Through her advocacy, mentorship, and commitment to social responsibility, she has created lasting change within her industry and beyond, helping pave the way for a more equitable and inclusive future.

The legacy that Emilie Kiser leaves behind is one of positive influence, not just through her professional achievements but through the values she has championed and the impact she has made on those around her. Her commitment to empathy, integrity, and personal growth has inspired countless others to lead with purpose and authenticity. Emilie's story is a testament to the power of resilience— the ability to navigate challenges, overcome adversity, and emerge stronger in the process. Her ability to stay true to her principles, even in the face of public scrutiny and industry pressures, is a reflection of the inner strength that has defined her path.

As Emilie's career continues to evolve, her influence will undoubtedly continue to grow, impacting future generations of leaders, innovators, and advocates. Her story reminds us that success is not solely about reaching professional milestones but about living a life that aligns with one's values, cultivating meaningful relationships, and making a positive difference in the world. Emilie Kiser's journey is far from over, and the legacy she has built will continue to inspire and guide those who strive to make a lasting impact—both in their industries and in their communities.

www.ingramcontent.com/pod-product-compliance
Lightning Source LLC
LaVergne TN
LVHW061555070526
838199LV00077B/7052